GREETINGS FROM WISCONSIN

Susan Lampert Smith

GREETINGS FROM WISCONSIN

Copyright ©1995 Susan Lampert Smith and the Wisconsin State Journal

Designer:
WENDY MCCLURE

Front Cover photo:
CAROLYN PFLASTERER

Section photos:
CAROLYN PFLASTERER
L. ROGER TURNER

Published by
Madison Newspapers, Inc.

Printed by
Straus Printing Company, Madison, WI
ISBN 1-878569-31-7

All rights reserved. No part of this publication may be reproduced or transmitted in any form or by any means, electronic or mechanical, including photocopy, recording, or any information storage or retrieval system without permission in writing.
For information,
contact Madison Newspapers, Inc., Marketing Department, P.O. Box 8056, Madison, WI, 53708.

*For Matthew,
who makes all things possible
and Ben and Lily*

Contents

CHAPTER 1
Wacky Wisconsin

	Page
Tick races	13
Performing bluegill	15
Gravity hill	16
Jury verdict	18
Go away	19
Yacht club	21
Baby hippo	24
JFK Jr.'s conception	25
Cuneiform fairy	27
Highsteppin'	28
Rose Bowl fans	32
Pagan rituals	34
Dark dungeon	35
Blessing the bock	37
Pasty prize	39

CHAPTER 2
Wisconsin People

	Page
Pearl Swiggum	43
Frank Zernia	48
Plain people	51
Joe McCarthy loyalists	53
Helen Broomell	55
The Jensens' angel	58
Jeanne Tregoning	59
Frank Zeidler	63
David Lowe	67
Patty & Ernie Get Married	70
Nell Peters	73
Gordon King	75

GREETINGS FROM WISCONSIN

CONTENTS *continued*

CHAPTER 3
Wisconsin Places

	Page
THE HOLY LAND	79
ROMANCE	82
THE HIGHGROUND	84
ST. PATRICK'S CHURCH	87
FIRST FISH FRY	89
GINSENG COUNTRY	90
BUFFALO RETURN	95
LAKE MILLS SLIDERS	97
HYMN SING	98
STRAWBERRY ISLAND	100

CHAPTER 4
Wisconsin Seasons

	Page
WINTER THAW-THE SMELLS OF WISCONSIN	105
WINTER THAW II	110
MUD SEASON	112
SUGAR CAMP	114
JELLO EASTER EGGS	116
MOTHER'S DAY 1993	118
MOTHER'S DAY 1994	120
DROUGHT BABY	122
HAYING SEASON SACRIFICES	123
LANGUISHING	127
WILD RICE	128
TURKEY TALK	131
NORWEGIAN CHRISTMAS	133
FIRETRUCKS FOR CHRISTMAS	135

INTRODUCTION

"Where are you calling from?"

The cranky voice on the other end belongs to an editor, who doesn't see me much.

"Romance? Where's Romance?

"You're in a bar, aren't you?"

Well, yes, where would *you* go looking for Romance? Actually, if you want to find it, Romance sits in a pretty little valley between Viroqua and the Mississippi River. And it has two taverns. And no, I don't always call in from taverns. It's just that my job involves roaming around the great state of Wisconsin. And much of Wisconsin is rural. And in rural Wisconsin, if you want to talk to people or use a phone, you have to go to the tavern. OK?

Actually, I understand why the office-bound editors get testy. Writing the Wisconsin State Journal's "On Wisconsin" column is a great job. One month I'm looking for Romance, the next I'm helping bless the bock beer in Milwaukee, the next I'm sipping maple syrup made the old way on the Lac du Flambeau reservation in far northern Wisconsin.

On many of these journeys I've travelled with State Journal photographer Carolyn Pflasterer, whose photos you'll find in this book and whose husband has given up asking why her car always needs to be washed after she's been out with me.

We've met some great Wisconsin people. You'll see the ghosts of a Milwaukee past when you walk the streets of the Inner City with Frank Zeidler, the city's last Socialist mayor. And you'll learn about the kind of sacrifice that holds our communities together when you meet the legend of Frank Zernia, an Adams County hero. Other people are impressive for their zest. For a trio of Wisconsinites who are living life with gusto into their 80s, I suggest you jump out of a plane with Gordon King, of Merrill, who parachuted into Normandy (again) in 1994 to celebrate the 50th anniversary of D-Day; paddle a canoe with Helen Broomell, of Minocqua, who's planning another solo canoe trip down the Yukon to mark her 80th birthday; and have a sleepover with beloved columnist Pearl Swiggum, of rural Vernon County, who square dances, plays a mean game of Scrabble and only shoots at blue jays to scare them.

Finally, Wisconsin seasons are so different and abrupt, it's like we live four entirely different lives. My favorite time of year is autumn as it winds down into winter, when life slows to a cozy circle of warmth around the woodstove, a perfect time for reading and playing cards. Summer is an orgy, when it feels as

GREETINGS FROM WISCONSIN

though you must: sail the Great Lakes, harvest a ripe tomato, go up North to hear the loons, grill brats, see baseball, water ski, camp, hike, bike, visit, and waterslide through the Dells or it won't really, truly be a Wisconsin summer. No wonder we need winter to recover.

The only Wisconsin season that makes me suffer comes along in March, the season of mud and gray skies. There's a column about that, too. Suffering must be good for us.

Mud season and all, I do feel romantic about Wisconsin. I can't imagine a better job than travelling the state's farm lanes and freeways.

I'm pleased to have you along for the ride.

Susan Lampert Smith
September 1995

Wacky Wisconsin

TICKS RACE IN NORTHWOODS DERBY
May 1995

OXBO — Think of it as the Northwoods version of the Kentucky Derby.

This past week, the Oxbo Resort on the banks of the beautiful Flambeau River hosted the 16th Annual International Woodtick Races.

Yes, woodticks. Those prehistoric creatures that crawl out of the trees and bury their heads in your scalp so as to better suck your blood. Ticks are actually cause for celebration here in the heart of the North, because their presence is the one sure sign that winter is truly over.

And celebrate they do at the Oxbo, a 1930s-style log cabin resort where the Flambeau rushes over a series of boulders. It's the kind of place that has an old metal Leinenkugel's Indian sign along the river, beckoning canoeists to come in and sip a cold one. It has a general store section that, in two feet or so of shelf, holds all the necessities of life: playing cards, Uncle Josh Pork Rind Bait, maple syrup, pickled pork hocks, and a big can of Permanone Tick Repellent.

One day a year, though, the ticks are the guests of honor.

Oxbo owner Dave Meyer said he inherited the tick tournament from the previous owners, although he's not sure how it all began.

"I'm sure it was after a few beers," he said. "They were probably picking ticks off themselves."

From such humble beginnings, an event of true Northwoods legends was born.

There was pageantry! The ticks arrived in Tupperware "trailers," carried by doting trainers. We met sisters Ginger Geng and Jean Wheeler at the door to the tavern and they were full of advice for novice tick racers.

"You have to keep 'em in your armpits," Wheeler said, demonstrating.

"Or between your legs," she said, not demonstrating. "They go a lot quicker when they're warm."

There was traditional food! Who needs mint juleps and Derby pie when you can have Miller on tap and Jean Meyer's "Tick Tacos?"

There were shady characters making a buck off a sporting event! An 11-year-old named Kipp Nordall, Park Falls, has for three years made money off a sure thing: Tick racers often forget to plan ahead. Kipp was at the bar, selling ticks from a big glass jar. This year the price was up to $1.50 each, on account of the cold spring weather.

And then there are the colorful names of the racers themselves. Forget Seattle Slew. I'll put my money on Tack-Tick, Tock-Tick, Loon-A-Tick, Moon-a-Tick, Epi-lep-tick and Take Down Your Pants. The last may sound like a strange name for a creature that doesn't, technically, wear pants. But it sounds great hollered in an encouraging manner by a crowd of beered-up tick racers.

And how, exactly, do ticks race?

The Tick International Speedway is set up on a pool table. The ticks are released in the center of a target and the one that makes it to the edge of the target first lives to race another round. The owner of the losing tick borrows the judge's gavel and sends the nonperformer to tick heaven with a satisfying THWACK!

There were some epic tick struggles. Geng's "Ms. Tickler," valiantly battled "Facial Tick" to victory, but the filly nearly lost her life in a case of mis-tick-en identity.

"Hey," Geng yelled, leaping to stop a losing opponent from hammering Ms. Tickler. "That's my tick, not yours!"

Attachments between ticks and people, though, are fleeting. A few rounds later, Ms. Tickler scrambled aimlessly and lost, and Geng slammed her into tick squish. Then Geng sat at the bar, cradling a drink with her gold glitter nails and murmuring sadly, "I can't believe I killed her. She was a good tick, and I killed her."

Things ended more happily for the two ticks that made it to the grand champion round. Winner Tom Graham, Spring Grove, Ill., ignored the crowd's cries of "Hammer! Hammer! Hammer!"

"No!" said Graham, tearily and beerily, of Moon-A-Tick. "It's like Free Willie. He's going back to the wild."

And runner-up Cindy Scott, Oxbo, refused to punish Try-N-Win for coming so close.

"I'm putting him out to stud," she said.

So if you're up in these parts next spring, you might stop and see if you can pick up the progeny of some proven winners.

Or you might just want to ask for a kid named Kipp.

Mr. Blue a Wisconsin Miracle
August 1995

YELLOWSTONE STATE PARK — As miracles go, Mr. Blue isn't a Madonna statue that weeps bloody tears or a flying saucer crashed into a cornfield.

But Mr. Blue the Performing Bluegill has one advantage — he's real. And he's just perfect for an end-of-August, lazy days of summer, Wisconsin kind of a miracle.

Mr. Blue was discovered back on Aug. 3, when Chris Prentice was cleaning up the rental boats at the Yellowstone Lake Chalet. Yellowstone Lake is near Blanchardville, about 45 miles southwest of Madison.

Well, it was August and the boats were full of dead crickets and so Prentice, 24, of Rockford, was chucking them into the water. Bluegills started swarming around to snap up a free breakfast. And one just started hanging around.

"First I got down on one knee and stuck the hand holding the cricket under the water and he took it out of my hand," Prentice says. "Next thing I knew he's jumping out of the water to get them."

Of course, getting a miracle to perform on command is another story. Prentice says his boss, Wayne "Fritz" Conrad, who has the concession to run the park's bait shop, didn't at first believe the Mr. Blue story.

"The first time my boss came down to see, he (Mr. Blue) wasn't around and I was like, 'Oh, man,'" Prentice says. "I started tapping my foot on the dock — and out he came from under the dock."

Since then, the sound of Prentice walking down the pier is enough to make Mr. Blue come swishing out of the shadows.

Prentice said his loyal fish has been there every day since Aug. 3, appearing in the early morning and sticking around until about 7 p.m., when he swims out for other parts of the 450-acre lake.

Conrad's wife, Arlene, has also fed Mr. Blue. And the park conservation warden has been down to videotape his miraculous performance.

Ranger Dick Black wrote in his daily log, "I have seen it, it is true."

And this is what a Mr. Blue performance looks like: Prentice kneels down on the pier, a foot or two from shore, and holds the cricket about a foot above the water. Soon, watchers from the shore can see the shape of a five-inch bluegill just below the surface, its dark eye fixed on the prize. Then there's a flapping and arching as the fish flings itself out of the water, its pursing lips aimed right at the cricket.

By the fifth or sixth cricket, Prentice must get closer to the water so Mr. Blue can daintily lift his head above the surface and suck up the bug.

If other bluegills try to horn in on the show, Mr. Blue chases them away.

Mr. Blue has almost become a pest.

"If I'm not going to feed him, I have to sneak down the other side of the pier so he doesn't see me," Prentice says.

"Otherwise, he comes up and looks at me with his mouth open."

Of course, such loyalty has a price.

As ranger Dick Black observes, "You could just hold a frying pan underneath and he'd jump right in."

Prentice worries that Mr. Blue will be easy prey for anglers (Conrad has made a 'no fishing' sign to hang near the pier) and for the muskie and northern pike that live in the lake's deeper waters.

"I'm afraid to feed him too much, because I'm afraid that when winter comes he won't know how to feed himself," says Prentice.

And so this winter, when the bait shop closes and the lake freezes over, you may start hearing strange stories from ice fishermen about a little fish that jumps up right through the ice holes.

And you'll know it's Mr. Blue.

And if, when the bait shop opens next spring, the sound of tapping feet brings a small shape out of the shadows of the pier, that will be a true miracle.

GRAVITY HILL THRILLS AND CHILLS
July 1994

SHULLSBURG — The banker, I am sure, didn't plan to spend his Thursday afternoon rolling backward on a county highway with me shrieking in the front seat next to him.

We were in Shullsburg to learn about serious things. About business expansions and historic districts for a story that - I promise - I'll write later.

It's just that when Jeff Russell, of the Clare Bank, was helpfully giving directions to our next stop he said, "Well, you go out of town past Gravity Hill...."

"Gravity Hill?" I interrupted. "Where strange forces of gravity suck cars backward up a hill?"

I should explain. I have this file, some of it in my head and some on tattered shreds of paper. All of them represent strange and wonderful places in Wisconsin that I one day hope to find.

I've stood on the north shore of Devils Island, the northwestern most of the Apostles, during a storm to hear the devils howl and suck in the lake caves that honeycomb the basement of the island. I've dragged my husband through the mosquito-infested Blue Hills near Rice Lake looking for the old Indian pipestone quarry. We found that, but not the Felsen Mer, a sea of rocks somewhere in the Blue Hills where the glacier filled a valley with giant boulders.

By now my husband is wise to the routine. I'll be peering at the map, saying, "If we turn at the next road we'll be right near a place where this huge spring gushes right out of a hillside. . . ." He just stomps the accelerator and drives on right past the turn.

I've been looking for Gravity Hill for years. But Jeff Russell is innocent of all this. So I put on the "PUL-EEZE Can I Have A Happy Meal?" pleading face that works so well for my children and soon we're headed south of town on Highway U.

Gravity Hill, Russell explains as he drives, is rediscovered by every generation of Shullsburg teen-agers. In fact, he figures that its initial discovery might have been by a romantic couple who started necking in a car parked near the bottom of Gravity Hill. Next thing they knew, they had rolled back uphill into Shullsburg, which is about 75 miles southwest of Madison in Lafayette County.

Let me explain. Or try to. A mile or two out of town, Highway U plunges down a good-sized hill, across a low area, and curves back up a steeper hill past Gratiot's Grove, a woods where early settlers made their fort.

Russell stopped his car about three-quarters of the way down the first hill, just short of a 25 mph sign that announced the curve back up the other side. From here, U appears to drop considerably to the valley floor before rising again.

Russell put the car in neutral and we began to roll, not into the valley in front of us but backward, slowly at first and then faster and faster. We were rolling up hill! The soybeans and wildflowers on either side of the road dropped below us as we rolled backward.

It was very cool. It may not be the Big Kahuna at Noah's Ark. But natural thrills are somehow more authentic.

So we did it again. Then we did it so Wisconsin State Journal photographer

Carolyn Pflasterer could take a picture of us doing it. Then we did it again so Carolyn, who thought she was along to photograph a totally different assignment, could ride along.

She agreed that it really was eerie. But on our next trip backward up the hill I noticed something worrying. It was Carolyn, crouching low in the soybeans. Now, Carolyn is a precise sort of person with one of those scientific minds. She is the kind of person who not only uses a computer, but actually understands it.

Carolyn had her face tilted flush with the road and was saying something about the whole scene being an optical illusion. "You can see where the road actually starts to level off right about here," she said.

I rolled up the window. I've already heard a better explanation from Russell. It seems that all the lead and zinc in the ground down here has created a sort of natural magnet, messing up the gravity and pulling cars up rather than down.

Exactly.

Now, I fix him with my best smile. Has he heard that there's an abandoned mine somewhere around here where a miner disappeared back in the heyday of lead mining and was never found? And can you still go down into this mine?

Last time I saw him, Russell was heading back to his bank as fast as he could legally drive.

JURY RULES ON COW JUSTICE
April 1993

DODGEVILLE — Threats to life and limb are a little different in Iowa County than in the city. And jurors here take a tough-minded view of how people should bear up under life's woes. Consider two jury trials that tied up the state's oldest courthouse for the past two weeks.

One that ended Friday after four days of testimony revolved around who let the cows out. And then there was the one about the snow on the jail roof.

The cow case ("A typical Iowa County case," commented Judge James Fiedler) concerned the events of Memorial Day Weekend 1988. Somehow, that hot Friday night, a wayward heifer and a minivan driven by a doctor from Omaha attempted to occupy the same lane of Highway 18-151.

The heifer lost.

The doctor's wife sprained her foot and sued.

And a jury judging Mineral Point farmer Larry Wolf was left to ponder:

Why Milwaukee attorney Larry Brueggeman kept referring to the heifer as a "black Angus beef animal?" Does that make the county's more common highway menace a "tan whitetailed venison animal?"

Why Brueggeman kept referring to them as both "folks" and "the collective conscience of your community?" And why Dr. Samuel Cohen's wife, Janet, who didn't work, might be entitled to $275,000 for loss of future income?

"We're here today, as mercenary as that sounds, to say we want fair and just money compensation," Brueggeman told the jury, in a county where per capita income is $11,339, that, all told, the Cohens deserved $743,000, in part because she "is essentially incapable of keeping up with Dr. Cohen's active lifestyle."

The jurors also heard from neighbors who said that Wolf was a good farmer whose cattle rarely got out. And that the same night, a neighbor hit another of Wolf's cows, wrecked his truck and didn't sue. And that Dr. Cohen might have been speeding.

"Larry Wolf is a good farmer," said defense attorney Claude Covelli of Madison. "That's not to say a calf can't squeeze through a fence. That's not negligence, that's being a farmer." But Brueggeman told jurors that if they excused an open gate, "you're saying you have a pretty relaxed view of responsibility."

The collective conscience of Iowa County thought about it for four hours and concluded Wolf wasn't a bad farmer. And so the Cohens got nothing. Which shouldn't give the impression juries in Iowa County are prejudiced against city folks.

A week before, another county jury stiffed one of their own. They sifted through 96 exhibits and four days of expert testimony about how longtime Iowa County dispatcher Richard Ehlert was leaving the county jail one January day, slammed the door and was beaned by a pile of snow, which wrecked his neck and strained his marriage.

And they apparently decided there was nothing wrong with the roof that looking up wouldn't fix.

So here, then, is today's message from Iowa County:

Snow falls down.

Cows get out.

So be careful out there — and don't expect to get rich.

Please go away
July 1995

MADISON — Oh, swell. In a year when Madison has hit the top of the lists for everything from outdoor activities to being the best place to raise kids, USA Today has to go and do a story on us being such a great place.

I know you don't take it seriously. These same publications were ripping us a few years ago for being the Tax Hell of the Rust Belt. Now they love all those things the hellish taxes pay for: good schools, clean lakes, parks.

But non-Cheeseheads could be reading this stuff and taking it to heart. And bad things happen to places that become trendy: congestion, Californians, shopping malls, Kurt Cobain. Do you really want to have to buy tickets to the Farmers' Market? Make reservations at Memorial Union? Sit next to Jack Nicholson at a Badger game? The stakes are high. It's time to begin dissing Madison before the place is ruined.

Actually, I've been at this for years. Whenever I meet people who ask me if Wisconsin is in Canada or refer to the Midwest as "flyover country," I heartily agree with them.

But I'm not so sure you're up to it. You might start blabbing about living on the lakes, the great Nepali restaurants or your kid's award-winning teacher and blow it for the rest of us.

So I want you to cut this out and keep it near the phone. This list is for when friends and relatives from far away call to ask how it is here in heaven. These are called "talking points." Spinmasters use them to keep candidates "on message." Remember, we're waging a campaign here to knock Madison out of the popularity polls.

Winter: This is an easy one. If you've ever been to the Sunbelt in winter, you know that half the newscast is devoted to footage of us benighted northerners shoveling head-high snow or sliding off bridge. Then a perky weathergirl comes on and announces, "But it was another beautiful day in sunny southern California..."

I know it's tough to remember winter in July, so just chant these phrases: "It gets so cold here the gas in your car turns to Jell-O. It gets so cold your nostril hairs freeze together. It gets so cold Wisconsin farmers buy special heaters to keep the manure from freezing solid before they spread it."

Taxes: Another easy one. Just make copies of your property tax bill and include them in all your holiday cards. Remember, the bills thoughtfully arrive just about the time that Santa does.

Fat: Yeah, yeah, we may have 800 softball teams, but we all go out for beer after the game. Madison may be trendy, but we're still part of the chubbiest state in the country.

Men should tell their out-of-state guy friends about "the Wisconsin triangle," a name coined by Eagle River writer Nell Peters for those enormous rear ends you see around here. I thought it was a hilarious term until I looked in the mirror and saw one following me.

And women, tell your out-of-state girlfriends what it's really like to be up close and personal with guys who live on bratwurst with kraut, fried cheese curds and beer.

Lutefisk: Don't tell 'em about it. Just send them some, fourth class, in the summertime. Enclose a little note explaining that it's "Wisconsin sushi" and that their kids have to eat it for breakfast everyday or they'll be teased in school.

Well, that's the short list. And here's a true life example of how to carry it off.

It was December 1993 and I was with 70,000 other Cheeseheads in Los Angeles to cheer our Badgers on to their Rose Bowl victory.

I don't know if it was my continental accent, my body shape or the beer in my hand at 10 a.m., but somehow the bus boy at our hotel just knew I was from Wisconsin.

He shook his head sadly and said, "I feel so sorry for you people. It's so cold there."

Did I get in his patronizing face and tell him that I'd rather live in a place that tops the list in college board test scores instead of one that's known for violent crime?

I did not. Instead, I gripped his tanned surfer arm with my pallid white hand and told him a sad, sad story.

All about how it got so cold, and the north wind blew so hard, that our water pipes froze solid. And then my husband set the insulation on fire trying to thaw them. And how my kids stood in the yard clutching their Christmas presents as the fire trucks tried to get through the snowdrifts.

"It's terrible," I said, snuffling into my Bucky cup. "You would HATE it."

YACHT CLUB NAVIGATES COUNTRY CHANGES
March 1994

ARENA — OK, so maybe Thomas Jefferson didn't have Porter's Restaurant or the Coon Rock Yacht Club in mind when he had all those ideas about creating a rural democracy.

But both institutions are worth visiting if you're interested in seeing how those ideas are faring in the last days of the 20th century.

If you make a visit to the back room, where there might be an animated discussion between two tables full of farmers and gentleman farmers — only the participants can tell the difference — about whether Americans will master the mysteries of grazing the way the Australians have.

"They know more about grass than we ever will," says farmer Paul Swenson, who's just back from the statewide grazing conference in Stevens Point. "They say the only way to learn about grass is to get down on their knees to see what it's doing."

At another table, you might find two tiny, gray-haired women eating field-hand-sized portions of corned beef and cabbage while they discuss who is sick and getting sicker and who else is sick but healing.

Up front, vegetable farmers Sonny Carson and Louis Carpenter are sharing a fast lunch with Mazomanie veterinarian Doc Schobert, who's between bovine patients and has just a few minutes to polish off a huge pressed-wood bowl full of boiled dinner.

Schobert orders (and pays for) a half order of the dinner. But after he leaves, Marion "Grandma" Porter confesses that she usually ignores what people say about how much food they want.

"I give them what I think they'll eat," she says.

Porter's is a little like having pie at Grandma's kitchen table while all the relatives drop by to gossip and chat. In fact, Porter's is located in two rooms tacked onto the front of Sonny and Marion "Grandma" Porter's home on a side street in Arena. The Porters have been in the restaurant business for most of the 46 years of their marriage.

"Forty-six years," Sonny observes, as he fills yet another coffee cup. "I could have killed two people, served two life sentences and been out on parole right now."

Some of the reasons Sonny has stuck with it surround him in the tiny, cluttered kitchen. The yeast rolls rising above a pan of warm water, the triplet loaves of homemade raisin bread cooking their brown backs on the stove, the crimped pie shell, waiting for Marion's time and inspiration.

"It might be pumpkin," she says, as she flips a pair of plate-sized pancakes. "It depends on how much time I have."

But it's more than Grandma Porter's great cooking that holds this place together. There's a chemistry of coffee and community that draws in even an outsider dining at Porter's.

There have been great ideas — and many more trivial ones — discussed in careful detail at these tables through the years. The Porters even have printed diplomas that bestow master's degrees in rural sociology from Porter University.

"We're going to have a graduation ceremony sometime soon," Marion says. "Some of these boys have been studying for a long, long time." The graduate seminar in rural sociology takes place most mornings at the front table. It is there that the Coon Rock Yacht Club holds its port-of-call meetings.

The farmers who started the yacht club don't have a rowboat among them. And the stream that rushes through Coon Rock valley holds barely enough water to float a bathtub flotilla. But the yachtsmen produce enough talk to float the Queen Mary.

It's a loose organization, although members can muster as many as 80 associates for a Christmas dinner or a rally of old-time, hand-clutch tractors. There are a few organizing symbols of the club. One is the spiffy white hats — with gold trim — worn by members on special occasions only, because the citified color scheme wouldn't survive its first encounter with manure or mud.

Another is the "breeding rock."

The namesake Coon Rock is a sandstone cliff that juts from one of the bluffs that line the south wall of the Lower Wisconsin River Valley. But the breeding rock is a boulder that grew out of yacht club admiral Tom Forseth's field. Since then, this dishwasher-sized chunk of rock has appeared, mysteriously, in Ron Andings' naturally rock-free valley farm and, lately, in a front yard across from the Congregational Church in Spring Green.

There's even a rock calendar, showing it dressed in a Father's Day tie for June, and as a turkey for November.

There are many stories to explain the breeding rock's wanderings.

"One story is that the university's been too busy creating new herbicides when what we really need out here is a rockicide," Forseth said. "Another story is that the high nitrate levels in the ground water keep pushing the rocks up from down below."

There is a certain dark side to the yacht club. Its name alone is a joking comment on the way rural society is heading.

Forseth said yacht club members know their farms are worth far more as recreational land for city people who actually own yachts than they are as farmland. Although he doesn't say it, many of the farms still left are supported by family members who work at Lands' End, selling boating clothes to people with real yachts.

So as former farms sprout $200,000 homes, and as yacht club members watch their new neighbors commute to jobs and shopping in Madison, the members cruise the currents of an older way of life.

"The real purpose is to discuss what we're trying to preserve here, with all the modernization taking place," Forseth says, between sips of Sonny Porter's coffee. "People used to share equipment, share work, raise barns together. Now we're becoming so isolated from each other."

A yacht club member who lives too close to the road risks a sprained neck from waving at all the cars that go by, Forseth says. He used to think city folks were stuck up, because they didn't wave back.

"But it's not that at all," he says. "It's just that they're so used to seeing people that they don't think they're anything special."

So the yacht club is really a tribute to neighbors, who still think it's something worth celebrating to have an hour to sit and sip coffee and sass each other. These are men who spend the rest of their days working alone, talking to themselves.

And so the organization chugs on, a 1943 John Deere hand-clutch club in an age of revved up super tractors. Sometime after the thaw and before the rush of spring field work, the yachtsmen will rally their old tractors in the Arena Park. There will be a lot of tinkering and razzing and an impromptu parade through the streets of town.

And then there will be a contest. But instead of a race, with the bragging rights going to the fastest, the yachtsmen will hold a backing-up contest and a "slow race" where they will honor the tractor that can creep forward at the most turtlelike pace.

That's a yacht club philosophy: slowing the pace of a fractured society, backing up to a time when community was still important. And laughing about it.

"Every small burb should have a yacht club," says Forseth, chugging the last of his coffee and getting ready to leave the warmth of Porter's for a cold March day of outside chores. "And a place like this where they can get together."

Hippo startles fishermen
May 1994

NESHKORO — You know fishermen and their stories — especially on a rainy Opening Day morning.

So, you can hardly blame Marquette County Lt. Gary Gardner when he got the call at dawn Saturday from the trout fisherman who claimed there was a dead hippopotamus in the Mecan River near Neshkoro.

"I kind of doubted it," Gardner said.

Gardner called Judi Nigbor, the state Department of Natural Resources warden for Marquette County and told her merely that there was a dead animal in the Mecan west of Highway 22. Nigbor wasn't too concerned.

"Every once in a while we get a complaint about a dead raccoon in the river," she said. "People see a dead animal and they want to know what it is."

So you can imagine her surprise when she got to Highway E and there it was: 1,700 pounds of dead hippopotamus, being hauled out of the Mecan River by a truck.

Now the Mecan is a clear-water stream that winds through Wisconsin's sand country, past pine trees and burr oaks. It is not Rudyard Kipling's great gray greasy Limpopo River all set about by fever trees.

And, when Nigbor inquired how this baby hippo from Africa came to rest in this curious spot, this is what she was told: The camel let it out.

At least that's what Mark Schoebel, the owner of Neshkoro's R-Zoo game farm, thinks happened. Until last week, the camel and the hippo lived at R-Zoo until someone (or something) opened the hippo cage.

Nigbor said the hippo wandered for two days — and at least 5 miles — before choosing this stretch of the Mecan in which to hunker. Nigbor said that Schoebel tracked the hippo after he discovered it missing. And when he found it Friday and couldn't get it out of the river, he shot it.

But before the stock truck got there, some trout fishermen rounded a bend on the Mecan Saturday morning and got the surprise of their lives.

"I heard that they took a picture of themselves standing on top of it," Nigbor said.

"We don't regulate hippopotamus," Nigbor said, "so there won't be a citation."

In 1986, Schoebel paid a $1,000 fine after pleading guilty to four federal violations. He was accused of supplying wild Wisconsin bears to Korea, where bear gall bladders fetch high prices as aphrodisiacs.

Now that the hippo has been determined to be really real — and really dead — Nigbor has been getting calls from people who will admit seeing it.

"People told me that by the time they saw it (standing in the creek), they would back up and look again and it would be gone. It probably went back underwater," she said. "It's not every day there's a hippopotamus wandering around Marquette County."

Was JFK Jr. conceived in Boscobel?
August 1994

BOSCOBEL — Some rumors are just so good they should be true.

And I must admit a certain fatal attraction to this one. After all, it contains all the necessary elements for great gossip: the late Jackie Kennedy Onassis, a hotel room, sex, religion, and Jackie's son, the world's most eligible bachelor.

Folks in Boscobel are by now rolling their eyes. This is, of course, the old "John F. Kennedy Jr. was conceived in Boscobel" rumor.

And it is a great rumor. It surfaced again this year when a candidate on the stump — shades of the pivotal 1960 Wisconsin primary! — was told that Boscobel was about to invite John F. Kennedy Jr. (John-John to people older than 40) to town to celebrate the renovations at the historic Boscobel Hotel.

So being a professional newsgatherer, I gathered all my sources of facts: tabloids, unauthorized Jackie O. biographies, and Shirley, who has the run of the morgue at the Boscobel Dial.

Now, Shirley has looked up the date of Jackie and Jack Kennedy's visit to

GREETINGS FROM WISCONSIN

Boscobel so many times she says she "ought to write it on the chimney."

Instead, it's in the dusty bound editions of the Dial for March 1960. Both John F. Kennedy and his archrival in the Wisconsin primary, Hubert Humphrey, visited Boscobel that week. There's no mention of the Kennedys checking into the Boscobel Hotel on March 25.

And Ralph Goldsmith, the Dial's longtime editor, concedes that the Kennedys went on to Eau Claire after an afternoon in Boscobel. But he says the Kennedys did check into a Boscobel Hotel room for a few hours to freshen up.

"I took a picture of the Kennedys — and they rented the hotel room for a short number of hours," says Goldsmith, who has given ink to this rumor himself a time or two in the past.

Like all oft-told tales, the story of those few fateful hours in the Boscobel Hotel has several versions.

As history buffs know, the Boscobel Hotel's Room 19 was where a pair of traveling salesmen started the Gideon Bible Society back in 1898. Now the Gideons make sure there is a Bible in every hotel room. Local author Ben Logan said he's heard a version of the Kennedy rumor that places Jack and Jackie in that historic room: "Some people say that it was the same room where the Gideons were born."

Now, here's where the serious finger counting starts. John F. Kennedy Jr. was born on Nov. 25, 1960, exactly 36 weeks after his parents spent an afternoon in Boscobel. Accounts from the time said that the 6-pound baby boy arrived three weeks before his expected due date. That puts us right in the Boscobel ballpark.

Now, Jackie spent much of the week before the Wisconsin primary campaigning on her own in Wisconsin, with Jack staying behind in Washington to cast a Senate vote on important civil rights legislation. As the rumor mongers have it, Boscobel was one of the few places the two were together that week.

So it is possible. Now, for the second part of the rumor: Is Boscobel preparing to invite John F. Kennedy Jr. back to visit the place where he might have been conceived?

Naahh, says Michael Riddet, a Boscobel artist and gallery owner, who added he "absolutely" wouldn't mind if Kennedy decided on his own to visit, especially if he brought along his sometime girlfriend Daryl Hannah.

Actually, Riddet said that a local group dedicated to saving the hotel is making progress without the help of the Kennedys or the Gideons. A few weeks ago, group members viewed an architect's plans for shoring up the 124-year-old hotel and making it accessible to people who use wheelchairs.

And on Oct. 8, the currently closed hotel will reopen to host 300 Civil War reenactors who will hold a "military ball with period embellishments" in the hotel. Money raised from that event will go to support Boscobel's Grand Army of the Republic Hall, one of the state's last G.A.R. halls.

So even if Boscobel doesn't attract JFK Jr., it will soon be hosting Robert E. Lee, Abe Lincoln and their armies.

And maybe John will take a cue from director and actor Ron Howard, who recently told US magazine (one of my trusty sources) that all of his children have middle names based on their points of conception.

"We have a Dallas. We have twin Carlyles, after the hotel," Howard said. "One son has a street name, but that's because Volvo isn't a very good middle name."

So think about it: John Fitzgerald Boscobel Kennedy. It kind of rolls right off the tongue.

Cuneiform fairy confounds Madison
October 1994

MADISON — Add to the list of Madison's exotic beings the mysterious "cuneiform fairy."

The fairy has been hiding his enigmatic offerings around Madison's lakes for several years now. Last week, Mark Kenoyer, an archaeologist at UW-Madison, put out a bulletin, alerting his colleagues to the fairy and his trickster ways.

Kenoyer gave his memo a title that sounds like Nancy Drew on a weird '90s trip — "The Mystery of the Cuneiform Tablet Fairy" — and in it, he describes his encounters with the artifacts left by this strange being. It seems that every once in a while, someone shows up at Kenoyer's office at the Social Sciences Building or over at the State Historical Society holding a small object for the archaeologists to identify.

Kenoyer said that each object is a small red clay tablet — "about the size of a Tootsie Roll" — inscribed all over with wedge-shaped symbols. The symbols are indeed part of the Sumerian alphabet used in the area that is now Iraq beginning in about 3000 B.C. So far, a few tablets have been found at Picnic Point on Lake Mendota. And about two weeks ago, a father appeared at the anthropology department holding another tablet his child found near Lake Monona.

"They're finding them on the surface, when they're looking for arrowheads," Kenoyer said.

Kenoyer said he congratulates people for having found a true artifact — not of ancient Mesopotamia but of modern Madison. He said that some mysterious person — he has a suspect in mind — is creating the clay tablets out of a brown stone ware clay and inscribing them using a stylus to make the symbols that make up either the ancient Sumerian or Akkadian alphabet.

"I have been able to identify letters," Kenoyer said. "The person who is doing this has gotten a book and is copying letters from the Sumerian alphabet."

Kenoyer didn't take the time to decipher the riddles, but thinks the tablets contain messages written in English using Sumerian letter sounds. Someone could decipher the message sent by the Cuneiform Fairy by getting a book on ancient writing.

Kenoyer said he didn't write his memo to be a spoil sport, but only to alert other archaeologists.

"I think it's a great idea for kids to find them and decipher them," he said.

That hasn't stopped him from trying to solve the puzzle. A few years ago at a State Street coffee house, Kenoyer spotted a guy manning the espresso machine who wore a bead made of the same brown clay and inscribed with the same ancient letters.

"I've been back to Steep & Brew and asked," Kenoyer said, "but no one seems to know who he is."

And that's as it should be. The mystery of the cappuccino-carrying Cuneiform Fairy can only help Madison hold on to its reputation as the Mesopotamia of the Midwest.

THAT HIGHSTEPPIN' WISCONSIN BAND
November 1994

COLUMBUS, Ohio — It is hours before game time, but the other contest between Wisconsin and Ohio State University is already under way.

On a practice lot in the shadow of Ohio Stadium, the two battling college bands are engaged in their first skirmish, a classic maneuver called the "psych-out."

The Ohio State band, dressed in military-style uniforms that haven't changed much since Herbert Hoover was president, stands rigid for inspection. As rank leaders march the rows, Ohio State band members snap to attention with a "ten-hut," and are slapped and patted to get their uniforms perfect. Hair hanging out of hat will be summarily snipped off; band members who haven't shaved will be fined.

From the Wisconsin gang, gathered 260 strong along a hill, comes a collective belch.

This is a group that looks like it has just rolled in from a hard night. Heads are topped with bandannas, dreadlocks or weird hair colors left from Halloween. Chins are scruffy, a direct pimp of Ohio State's shave or pay rule. The trombone players are wearing nothing but boxer shorts. When Wisconsin takes to the practice field to warm up, they greet Director Mike Leckrone with chants of "Hurt me, hurt me, hurt me."

Their goofy calisthenics look like something from the Bill Murray movie "Stripes."

But once they finally put horns to lips and play, the sound is brash enough to flatten the Buckeye band back against the hill. And the Ohio Staters are soon singing along with the Wisconsin band's Wilson Pickett number.

After practice, the Wisconsin band huddles around their drum major, pixie-like former clarinetist and Marinette High School valedictorian Beth De Kelver, who leads the band in a chant of "Let's rip their hearts out with a spoon."

Then the drummers begin a soft tattoo as Leckrone launches into what long-time band members call his "God Save America speech."

"There are many differences between these two bands," Leckrone intones, "and the most important one is that when you're out on the field you're going to have Fun!"

The band roars and charges off the practice field. The only thing left behind is a scarlet Ohio State T-shirt, ripped to shreds and ground into the asphalt by 520 high-stepping feet.

Yes, pack up the ladies and lock your hotel doors, the Wisconsin Marching Band is on a road trip. This once-a-year trip is a chance for band bonding and to show off for another Big Ten crowd. They've wowed them in Iowa and had them chicken dancing in their seats in Michigan.

But things are changing for the band. Last year, Playboy magazine named it the best college band and it rocked the Los Angeles area during the Rose Bowl, winning a headline that read "The University of Wisconsin Band....Yes, It Was Better Than UCLA, Too." So there is more notoriety.

But the biggest change is probably the fact that the band is now accompanying a respectable football team. (As a Denver Post wag put it, "Wisconsin finally has a football team that the band can be proud of.")

In the past, the band's famous "Fifth Quarter" was celebrated by the media in the cities Wisconsin visited. They were amazed by the happy cheeseheads, good sports who were too dumb to know or care that they had just lost a game. Win or lose (and it was usually lose) the Badger fans would be rolling out the barrel, chicken-dancing and yodeling the Bud Song long after the home fans were gone.

But after 17 years of Fifth Quarters, things are different.

"What we're finding with the Fifth Quarter is that people take it differently with a winning team," Leckrone says, as he watches the Ohio State band practice. "With a winning team, people see it as taunting."

And these Ohio State fans can't take a taunting. After being thoroughly whipped the previous week by Penn State, they can barely talk about Ohio State football and Coach John Cooper without their facial muscles twitching and the veins in their necks bulging. These people are in no mood for the Bud Song.

Before the practice, Ohio State Band Director Jon Woods greets Leckrone warmly, but asks him to keep his band on his side of the field during the Fifth Quarter and to stop Wisconsin band members from scampering around the stadium to play to the opposing band.

"Our fans," Woods tells Leckrone, "are a little sensitive."

An hour later, the Wisconsin band has been transformed. All traces of scruffiness have disappeared beneath the band's new red and white uniforms. Tubas gleam and the whole band looks sharp as it marches into St. John's Arena for a pregame "skull session" with the Ohio State Band.

Like everything at Ohio State, the "skull session" is a tradition that dates back decades. Since the Ohio State band — unlike Wisconsin — plays its tunes by memory, a long-ago band director decided members would benefit from a final, pregame concert to drum the music into their skulls. And because Ohio State invites another band to nearly every home game, the session is a pregame band playoff and a chance for some 10,000 fans to observe other bands.

To Badger fans who've never seen another band, the competition seems a little dull. A book called "Big Ten Country" ranked the Ohio State and Wisconsin bands as the two best in the Big Ten. But comparing the two is like comparing the Mormon Tabernacle Choir to the Tina Turner Revue — both are good at what they do and put out a lot of sound, but only one gets you boogieing on your chair.

The Ohio State band bills itself as the Best Damn Band In The Land and it does sound like a perfectly tuned concert band both on and off the field. For the skull session, Ohio State plays a very lovely version of Strauss' "Also sprach Zarathustra" — the "2001: A Space Odyssey" theme — and the same Ohio State classics they perform for every show.

Then it's the Wisconsin band's turn. Their "Also sprach Zarathustra" is a rowdier version, known locally as "Space Badgers," and contains several "On, Wisconsin" riffs. So does the "1812 Overture," which Leckrone introduces as being written by "Badger and South Milwaukee native Pete Tchaikovsky." Leckrone introduces the Badgers' version of the Buckeye Battle Cry as "the Nutcracker Suite," much to the non-amusement of the Ohio State fans, many of whom wear lumpy brown necklaces of Buckeye nuts around their necks.

One Buckeye fan, dressed in the grim gray of Ohio State, turns to another and says, "This is a very, very disruptive group. They have the worst reputation in the Big Ten."

Then his voice drops to a tone of disbelief: "Most people go to a game to watch football. People there go to a game to drink and have fun and watch the band."

Later at Ohio Stadium both bands look great. Ohio State does its trademark Script Ohio maneuver — which looks like meaningless marching from the ground but eventually spells out Ohio and dots the "I" with a tuba. The crowd, despite having seen this trick at every game for decades, goes wild.

The reasons the Wisconsin band looks so great on the field may not be apparent to casual band fans. There are the uniforms, which dramatically flip from red fronts to white backs as the band whips through its turns, there is that jerky, "stop-at-the-top" high step, difficult to perform but exciting to watch. But mostly it's the "in-your-face" energy the band blows out through its music.

The band has been working toward this Ohio State performance since August. Because of Ohio State's reputation for excellence — and because it videotapes the opposing band's performance — Leckrone's legendary perfectionism has been ratcheted up a few notches.

"Watch your feet!" he's been yelling at practice all week. "They will."

At half-time, the Wisconsin band pours onto the field and launches into the soundtrack from "Forrest Gump." They march through milestones of popular music, from Elvis to Three Dog Night, and finish with a flourish on "Turn, Turn, Turn" by the Byrds.

Unfortunately, the football team gives the band little to honk their horns about. After the Badger's 24-3 defeat, satisfied Ohio State fans stream out of the stadium, leaving behind about a thousand cheeseheads and a handful of Ohio State fans who know about the Fifth Quarter.

Buckeye fan Chris Lewie, a county planner from Springfield, Ohio, cheers as the Wisconsin trombones, dressed in their spiffy new red and white rain coats, surround two Columbus police officers during "Space Badgers." Lewie says he stuck around because he had seen the Wisconsin band when they were in town three years before.

"I couldn't believe a 3-and-8 team would do something like that," Lewie said, demonstrating a Buckeye-like memory for football statistics. "They're a very, very exciting band and we have a very, very conservative band."

His friend Eric Phillips agrees, adding, "Your band makes our band look anal retentive."

After watching highlight clips of their half-time and pregame performances in the Ohio State band room inside the stadium, the band finally marches out of the stadium, across Woody Hayes Drive and back to their buses.

As they do in Madison, where they march down the bike lane of University Avenue after home games, the band makes its exit a performance. They get applause from Buckeye and Badger fans along the street. A car that stopped to let them pass honks along with the Bud Song.

Back at the buses, the band takes part in the same sort of closing ritual it usually does in the courtyard of the Humanities Building. After singing a soft and slow "Varsity," arms clasping shoulders and swaying together, the band leans close so that drum major De Kelver can cheer their performance. Then she shouts her final order of the trip, a line from the Wang Chung hit "Everybody Have Fun Tonight": "Everybody Wang Chung tonight!"

And, back at the hotel, they do.

AND THOSE WILD ROSE BOWL FANS
January 1994

PASADENA, Calif. — A new kind of smog licked at those mansions atop the San Gabriel mountains Saturday. It was a little spicy, a little greasy and carried with it the smell of a thousand brats grilling.

Maniac Badgers fans turned Arroyo Boulevard into Breese Terrace Saturday. They tailgated, they drank beer, they painted big Ws on their naked chests. And inside, the Rose Bowl looked like Camp Randall Stadium. All but a few sections of the stadium blazed Badgers red. After the victory, only a few rows of fans left as the UW Marching Band's polkas turned the Rose Bowl into a rural Wisconsin beer hall.

"Boy, do you have a lot of fans here," said Dan Griese, son of ABC sportscaster Bob. Griese the younger, a UCLA fan, estimated that 80 percent of the fans were from Wisconsin. "I've been to four UCLA Rose Bowls and I've never seen an opposing team crowd like this."

Indeed. Despite the ticket scandal, there were tickets to be had outside the gate and tens of thousands of Wisconsin fans inside.

Before the game, Karl Hansen, UW Class of 1986, believed it was his destiny to see the Rose Bowl. So he was comfortable turning down a pair of $200 tickets for himself and his sister Mary, a UW-Madison sophomore.

"I'm not paying that," he said, waving off the ticket scalper. "It'll get cheaper at kickoff."

Hansen had reason to believe. He was celebrating his 31st birthday Saturday and had the driver's license to prove it.

That's right. On the day he was born, the Badgers were playing in their last Rose Bowl.

Nearby, John Kohl, of Brentwood, was more than willing to pay the price. "These are the best fans I've ever seen," said Kohl, who not only switched loyalties from his neighborhood team, the Bruins, but even went so far as to buy a

Wacky Wisconsin

"Mr. Polkaholic" tape from the Wisconsin party.

Before the game, the lawn of the stadium was like a Homecoming party.

Here were Ken and Jill Werner, the Milwaukee couple who were married on the field at Camp Randall stadium on Sept. 14, 1991. Ken was wearing his formal bridegroom tuxedo jacket (with Bucky embroidered on the back) with the brightest pair of red on white Badgers pants this side of Jingles Bar.

"Mike Leckrone gave them to me as a wedding present," he said.

There was Jim "Murph" Murphy, owner of the Riley Tavern, standing under a palm tree and sipping a beer, a beautiful smile on his face.

And coming across the Brookside Country Club golf course, which rings the back side of the Rose Bowl, was Barbie Schmock, of Madison's favorite food family (Smoky's and Barbie's Baked From Scratch cookies), resplendent in glittering red sequins over a pair of Bucky Badger boxer shorts.

"We're having a GREAT time," she said, saying Badgers fans have been having a weeklong party at the Venice Bistro Bar on Venice Beach.

And there were cow hats, cheeseheads and cheese hats everywhere.

Under one of the cheese hats was Andrew Dickler, a '90 graduate of UW-Madison who now lives in Los Angeles. With him was Steve Kriozere, a '91 graduate, who was holding a sign that said, "Barry Alvarez Says: Eat Cheese Or Die."

During the game, the student section exploded with "BARE-EEE, BARE-EEE," whenever Alvarez ventured onto the field.

During halftime, it seemed the whole stadium stood for the UW Marching Band's medley of rock favorites. Even Rose Queen Erica Brynes waggled her royal rear to the band's version of James Brown's I Got You (I Feel Good.)

But in the last 3 minutes, the party in the stands turned into a group tension headache as the Bruins threatened to deny the fans who had waited so long.

"Stop talking to me until we win," Lorene Persons, Eau Claire, admonished his daughter, Lezlyn, and niece, Mandy.

The stands erupted when time ran out. A thousand flashbulbs winked as the team took its victory lap and tears streamed as the stands rocked to "Varsity" and multiple versions of the "Bud Song." Twenty minutes later, when the fans finally started filing out, Arlie Mucks stood outside the gate, wearing a hat with a furry badger on it and a big smile.

Mucks took over the Wisconsin Alumni Association 32 years ago, when the Badgers were getting ready to go the last Wisconsin Rose Bowl. He hung on through the lean years.

And as New Year's night set in, the fans who waited so long waited to shake his hand.

"Thousands of people worked for this and there's not a more deserving group," Mucks said. "Elroy Hirsch and I went to more than 7,000 Badger events over the years and we always said, 'Wait 'til next year.' "

"Next year is here."

Madison's Famous Pagan Rites of Spring
March 1995

MADISON — It might be that the early thaw has us confused, but Madisonians had better get moving on our annual pagan rites.

If you need instructions, here is how Madison businessman Ted Lisse described our annual festival of Spring to one of his fraternity brothers from Northwestern University in a letter a year ago: "Living in Madison, as I do, among the descendants of the Huns, Vikings and Slavs, during the Ides of March I find myself subject to many strange customs brought on by the area's peculiar weather anomalies.

"Each March, two days before the vernal equinox and coinciding with the worst snowstorm of the year, the local natives, descendants of some pretty hearty, barbaric Indo-European tribes, carry their dried Christmas trees to a large communal field where the trees are stacked into one tremendous pile.

"The next day, at the designated hour of 10 p.m., after spending all day with family and friends at their favorite pubs, the locals, armed each with a bottle of world-famous Wisconsin brandy, proceed like lemmings on their march to the sea, to a special field where the humongous pile of Christmas trees is doused with the brandy and set afire.

"Howie, you'll never believe what these loveable Cheeseheads do next!

"They strip to the waist, every last one of them — man, woman, child — and dance bare-chested around the huge bonfire until it turns to embers. And, if that isn't enough, the yahoos use the embers to roast their brats. Then, as the sun's first rays peak above the eastern horizon, they crack open the kegs of beer that have been left in snow drifts to cool off and toast the new Spring season."

Ted then invited Howie to participate in this year's festival by visiting the Lisses at their condo on Lake Mendota "which has a breathtaking view of the ice fishermen struggling to stay afloat on the last patches of winter ice."

Ted Lisse died on Christmas Day, at age 59, of fast-moving bladder cancer. And when his wife, Richie, started getting condolence notes, she got one from Phi Ep brother Howie, indicating he thought the spring festival was real, and had been planning on coming to this year's party.

Richie said she thinks last year's Rose Bowl publicity, with Cheeseheads doing strange things in view of national television cameras, led Howie and others to believe that anything was possible in Wisconsin.

"He was a great guy," Richie said, of her jokester husband. "I really miss him."

Ted was a familiar figure, either at the family's Madison Computerworks store on Whitney Way, or windsurfing and rollerskating (never blading) near their Middleton condo or swimming at Harbor Athletic Club. He loved Madison with the fervor of an adopted son.

So, on this, the first full day of Spring, strip to the waist, burn a Christmas tree, roast a brat, and raise a chilly toast to the end of winter in these parts.

Ted Lisse would like it.

COUNTY DUNGEON KEEPS ITS SECRETS
April 1995

DODGEVILLE — Despite the roaring and beeping of backhoes behind the Iowa County Courthouse these days, the county's dark and scary "dungeon" will survive progress and live on into the 21st century.

Construction began a few weeks ago on the $2.3 million addition to the state's oldest courthouse. So far, the result is a giant crater, but standing on the edge of it, waiting to be incorporated into the new building, is one of the state's oldest jails. This limestone block was built in 1870, a decade after the courthouse. And in the basement is the dreaded dungeon, the place where Iowa County put its worst more than a century before anyone coined the phrase "super max" prison.

Now, Iowa County hasn't used the building as a jail since the current jail was built out on Highway 18 decades ago. But the dungeon is still there, in all its creepy glory.

You go through a door helpfully labeled "dungeon," and down some very steep stairs, through a basement, then pull open a heavy wooden door, and then you're in the dungeon.

The dungeon features about six cells. The cells are made of solid rock, with no windows or doors. Prisoners were presumably stuffed through small openings about six feet off the floor and dropped into the cells, where they were left in the dank dark to contemplate their wrongs.

County Zoning Administrator Ken Palzkill is one of many county employees who have visited the dungeon and heard tales about it.

"I've heard it was used for the people who were considered uncontrollable," Palzkill said. "It wasn't used for the guy who stole a pig. It was for what used to be called 'the criminally insane.'"

And, if they weren't insane going in, they probably were coming out.

One of Iowa County's most celebrated criminals may have died there. Dodgeville historian Gerald Fieldhouse said he has wondered whether the "mad servant" who allegedly killed Frank Lloyd Wright's mistress, Mamah Cheney, and six others and burned Taliesin in 1914 died in the dungeon.

The servant, Julian Carleton, was described by Wright as "a thin-lipped Barbados Negro" burned the estate to cover up his murders. Wright, who was in Chicago working on Midway Gardens at the time of the murders, described the aftermath of the crime in his autobiography:

"The madman was finally discovered hiding in the firepot of the steam boiler, down in the smoking ruins of the house. Still alive, though nearly dead, he was taken to the Dodgeville Jail."

When Carleton died in jail seven weeks later, his cause of death was listed as starvation. Accounts from the time say Carleton swallowed hydrochloric acid in a suicide attempt, and spent the last weeks of his life slowly dying, his mouth and throat so burned he could neither eat nor talk.

Despite the stories, Fieldhouse said he has never come across hard evidence that the dungeon was used.

"I've gone through an awful lot of county board records and I've never seen any reference to anyone being put in the dungeon," he said.

The regular jail was on the main floor and the sheriff had his home and office in an attached annex that bulldozers knocked over when construction began. Fieldhouse said he thinks sheriffs used the dungeon mostly as a threat.

Whatever its use, when the Iowa County Board finally voted to add offices to the courthouse — its first addition since 1947 — it also voted to preserve the old jail for historical reasons.

County employees seem happy about it. Greg Evans, whose Soil Conservation Service Office shared the old jail with the dungeon for 28 years, said he's taken countless visitors downstairs for a flashlight tour of the old cellblock. Once he shimmied up the wall and peeked inside.

"I saw an old tin can with the top cut off, like they just threw it in there for someone to eat," he said. Once construction moves into the old jail, Evans' office will move elsewhere.

"I'll miss the old dungeon," he said.

County Chairman Dick Scullion said the new addition will connect the current courthouse to the old jail and be faced in limestone to match the two old buildings. The old jail will become a meeting room on one level and a break room for employees.

But the dungeon will remain, lurking beneath the county's new offices like a dark secret from the past.

MILWAUKEE BLESSES ITS BOCK BEER
March 1994

MILWAUKEE — In San Diego they bless the fleet, in Milwaukee during Lent they bless the beer.

The Sixth Annual Blessing of the Bock Sunday drew more than 500 home-brewers, microbrewers and others with a religious passion for good beer to the Milwaukee County War Memorial.

There they brought their home-bottled dopplebocks and brewery-produced Mai bocks to the front of the Memorial Hall so the Rev. Guy Gurath of St. Casimir's Catholic Church could bless them all.

"To be honest," the priest told the crowd, "I forgot the holy water. But once I bless the beer, it will all be holy water."

Gurath wrote a poem for the occasion, which began:
"Dear Lord bless this bock
As we gather here at one o'clock
It is your gift of barley and hop
though, for some, it packs quite a sock
So, it is true, some should be total abstainers
But the rest of us can remain happy retainers
For even in the Book of Genesis, scholars agree
The problem was the pair on the ground,
Not the apple in the tree."

Afterward, Gurath said he found nothing unusual about blessing beer. When he was a priest in San Diego, he said, he would bless the U.S. Navy fleet before it left port. Priests bless animals on feast of St. Francis and cars on the feast of St. Christopher, the patron of travelers.

"If I was a Baptist I wouldn't be here," Gurath said, noting that bock beer has its roots in Roman Catholic Lenten traditions.

Because monks fasted and abstained from meat during the 40 days of Lent that lead up to Easter, the monastery breweries would brew bock beer to drink during the season. Bock — German for goat, symbolizing its strength — is a richer, heavier beer brewed with more grain, so it has more protein and alcohol.

The famous Paulaner Monastery brewery in Germany traditionally tapped its bock on March 19, the feast day of its patron St. Joseph.

And while St. Joseph isn't the patron of beer, Gurath said saw other links to the feast day.

"He is the patron saint of the happy death," he said, "so if you have a beer in one hand and a rosary in the other, that could be a happy death."

The Blessing of the Bock festival began five years ago. Jim Klisch, a founder of Milwaukee's Lakefront Brewery and a parishioner at St. Casimir's, approached the church about reviving the old tradition after seeing a picture of an Irish priest blessing beer and finding a beer blessing in the Catholic "Book of Blessings."

The event began at the Stork Club, a Milwaukee tavern.

"I thought it was going to be a flop," said Klisch, as he tapped Lakefront bock and Riverwest stein beer for thirsty masses. "I was sitting in the bar 10 minutes before it was supposed to start and there's no one there. Then a busload of home-brewers from Madison pulled in and filled up the bar. They started the festival."

The blessing outgrew the Stork Club, moved to St. Casimir's and outgrew the church hall in two years and now fills two floors of the War Memorial on Milwaukee's lakefront. In recent years, the event has been a fund-raiser for Highground, the Vietnam veteran's memorial near Neillsville.

John Zutz, who works for Lakefront Brewery and is on the Highground board, organizes the event with the help of about 100 volunteers.

On Sunday, hundreds of beer lovers paid $20 — or $10 plus a six pack of home-brewed beer to share — for a chance to sample beers from 18 regional breweries and from dozens of home-brewers.

It is sobering, or perhaps intoxicating, to realize that such a gathering couldn't have taken place a decade ago, even in the city that beer made famous.

Back then, the American beer scene was dominated by a handful of giant breweries and their low-cost, pallid brews. But since Milwaukee's Sprecher Brewing company opened in 1985, Wisconsin has seen a renaissance of small local breweries.

At Sunday's gathering, beer drinkers could sample Oatmeal Stout from Gray's Brewing in Janesville, Uff-Da Bock from the New Glarus Brewing Co., Dopplebock from Middleton's Capitol Brewery and Calumet Dark from Rowland's Calumet Brewing Co. in Calumet, to name a few.

One hot item was the "Neck Glass," a plastic, hourglass-shaped flask that hangs from the beer drinker's neck, leaving the hands free for holding bratwurst and gesturing.

Wacky Wisconsin

Everyone's an Expert When It Comes to Pasties
March 1995

FENNIMORE — Forget the Oscars. There was controversy, tension and talk of scandalous dress aplenty in southwest Wisconsin on Tuesday during the awarding of the "Cornys" to the winners of the first-ever Perfect Pasty Bake-off.

What, you flatlanders ask, is a pasty? First of all, it's pronounced PASS-tee, not PASTE-tee, which are those those spangly things strippers (and some Oscar nominees) use to cover their nipples.

Eventual Corny winner Dale Eggers, executive chef at the Timbers Restaurant in Platteville, said the cooks there always have fun with the new college student waitresses, who, when they come into the kitchen to order their first PASTE-tee, are told, "They usually come in pairs."

Secondly, we can tell you that a real pasty originated with the Cornish miners who flooded this area during the lead mining boom of the 1830s. They liked taking these turnovers of meat and potatoes down into the mines with them, to eat as their midday meal. Because of the way they were eaten, pasties were called "Cornish harmonicas."

And, although the mines are long closed, pasties remain a regional specialty in this part of the state.

On Tuesday, chefs from the Arrow Inn in Lancaster, the Brewster Cafe in Shullsburg, the Courthouse Inn in Dodgeville, the Red Rooster Cafe in Mineral Point, Narveys Restaurant in Dodgeville and the Rountree Restaurant and the Timbers, both of Platteville, put their pasties on the line.

The winner, the Timbers, walked off with the Corny, a statue created and donated by celebrated Muscoda junk sculptor Ellis Nelson depicts a squirrel swiping a pasty and is entitled "Cornwall steals a pasty." The smaller second-place statue, "Corny steals a pasty," was awarded to the Rountree Restaurant, and the third place "Little Wally steals a pasty," went to Narvey's.

Even competing in the contest, sponsored by the Points of Beginning Heritage Tourism Project, takes some hubris. As Jeff Lutes, manager of the Brewster Cafe, said, "Everybody in southwest Wisconsin grew up eating them."

The churches here don't have bake sales, they have pasty sales. The IGA store in Mineral Point sells what is called "pasty meat," coarsely ground beef just the way some (but not all) cooks like it.

Almost every essential ingredient of the pasty is open to debate.

Patti McKinley of the Red Rooster uses chopped steak, Catherine Paquette of the Brewster uses cut up tenderloin tips, Ken Elowson of Narvey's favors ground beef. Potatoes and onions are agreed on, but only some people will put in rutabagas or carrots. (Peas are seen as a Michigan perversion and won't even be discussed in polite company.) McKinley's mom, Helena Lawinger, and Paquette, both cook up delicious homemade chili sauces, but Paquette will also serve hers with gravy.

"NOO-OOH!," said Rachel Bunker, of the Arrow Inn, on the gravy controversy. "That would be an insult."

And, because Bunker's Welch and Cornish grandfather used to take real pasties down into real lead mines, where he kept them warm on a real potbelly stove, we must listen to her.

Actually, Mark Knipping of the Pendarvis Historical Site suggested some of the contest pasties may have been a bit too flaky in the pastry to qualify as authentic. He related the story of the French bride who thought she'd treat her husband to a delicate pasty for his lunch at the mine.

"He said it was no good, that it fell apart in his pocket," Knipping said. "The ones his mother made, you could drop to the bottom of the shaft without breaking."

Knipping noted that pasties are found from the Lake Superior Iron Range to California. Anywhere there was mining, there were Cornish mining supervisors and Cornish pasties.

Pasty making, he said, is "very much a family or local tradition, so what seems right to one person may not be how they make them in the next town or the next valley."

All pasties trace their origin to the poverty of Cornwall, Knipping said, where people made their food stretch by making pies out of eels, stillborn calves and entrails. One Cornish pie used the herring-like pilchards and a top crust that was cut, so the fish heads would poke out and gaze heavenward with their sightless eyes, giving it the name "Starry Gazey Pie."

Knipping said potatoes (which came to Cornwall from the Americas) and beef (a symbol of growing Cornish prosperity) were relatively new ingredients in Cornish pies when the Cornish immigrated to southwest Wisconsin.

A panel of judges sampled and debated the merits of the seven pies, before awarding the Cornys.

Besides his statue, Eggers and the Timbers won the right to defend the honor of the pasty against pretenders from the Iron Range in a competition in Hurley in May. Eggers said the award is an honor and vindication for the 24 years elderly women have been stopping by to tell him he makes pasties the wrong way.

"We get some real purists," he said.

And there was some speculation that people up in Hurley, being on the border of Michigan, may have some very strange ideas about what goes into a proper pasty.

Shirley Kort, a Cassville woman who organized Tuesday's competition, recalled an elderly woman of her acquaintance who went to Michigan and was served one of those unholy pea-spiked pasties: "She told them, 'This might be your idea of a pasty, but it's not mine.'"

Wisconsin People

The World is Pearl's Oyster
March 1995

TOWERVILLE — Pearl Swiggum doesn't sound all that surprised when we ask if we can visit Stump Ridge Farm. Or when we add that, well, there might be a lot of us.

When I mentioned I was doing a story on Pearl and her upcoming book, half the Wisconsin State Journal copy desk begged to go along. After all, they have an unofficial fan club called "Pearl's Girls," and fight each week over who gets the honor of editing her column for Monday's State Journal.

So that is how we came to be sitting like six dutiful granddaughters around

Pearl's round oak table, looking at old pictures and eating watercress sandwiches.

Actually, Pearl is used to this. Besides the State Journal, her column appears in the Crawford County Independent, the Boscobel Dial and the Mason City (Iowa) Globe-Gazette, so she regularly gets letters, poems and gifts from strangers. And a couple of times a week, unfamiliar cars drive slowly along Stump Ridge, their drivers looking for Pearl's mailbox.

"They say they want to meet me," she says, bustling, as always, around her kitchen. "But they usually talk about themselves."

The reason may be that they feel like they're part of a one-sided friendship. Each week they get a letter from Stump Ridge that is like a friendly note from a wise grandmother or a longtime friend.

They know all about Pearl. Her ongoing battle with hawks and blue jays, her free and wild childhood in the country, her grief over losing her husband of 50 years and, just this last summer, her loyal dog, Boots. They know that she gets lost whenever she leaves home and that she likes hugging men more than women.

And so, they reason, she must want to know all about them.

Perhaps they come to Stump Ridge in northern Crawford County to see if it looks like she described it.

And it does.

There's the outdoor telephone. And there are the barn cats: Puff, the fluffy caramel one, and Groucho and Wheezy, the black ones that Pearl worries (with a farm wife's unsentimental kindness) might be morons. There's the step ladder, erected to discourage hawks from swooping through the yard to snap up feeding songbirds.

Inside the house, there are the birthday presents sent well in advance of her 81st birthday on March 24, because her family knows she likes the anticipation of having wrapped gifts around the house. And there's the wrapped and ribboned "flu package," assembled each year by daughter Marjie Jurgensen. It can't be opened ahead of time — lest the transgressor be struck ill just by touching it — but if last year is any guide, it contains chicken soup, tea, honey, cold pills and at least two shots of brandy.

There's no sign of the gun, which Pearl has used to scare away the aggressive jays. That column inspired a spate of anti-Pearl letters, including one from a writer calling her a "speciesist," apparently sort of a bird racist.

"I didn't say I shot the blue jays," Pearl says, sounding exasperated. "I said I shot at them. I never could hit them."

If any writer can evoke a sense of place, it's Pearl. And her authority comes from having lived here for most of the century. Except for a few teen-age years attending high school in La Crosse and teacher's college at the Normal School in Viroqua, Pearl has lived her whole life within walking distance of Towerville. To hike with her down off the ridge and into the deep valley that Tainter Creek has cut into the Kickapoo hills is to watch the events of all those years come alive at once.

Down the ridge we pass the white Victory school, now the home of one of Pearl's nephews and his family. But 70 years ago, it was where Pearl and her eight siblings comprised half the school. And a few years later, it was the scene of Pearl's one, unglorious year as a school teacher. ("I was a terrible teacher," says Pearl, who always wanted to be a farmer.)

Down deeper in the valley, the Towerville Tavern was once the general store of handsome Norwegian immigrant Seeger Stevenson, Pearl's father. Exotic bananas hung in the picture window and children played in the creek out back.

Across from the store, on a rise, stood the house where Pearl and her siblings were born. It burned down years ago. But if you stand on the rise and look across Tainter Creek valley to where the hills begin to lift again, you can see the cemetery where Pearl's mother, Goldie Davis Stevenson, is buried. She died, pregnant with a sixth child, in the terrible flu epidemic of 1918. Her mother, Pearl's grandmother, died of flu the next week.

Pearl, who was 3, has no memory of her mother. She and her siblings were raised in the house across from the store by a pair of stepmothers. The first whipped the children. The second, Pearl says, was worse.

"She was a belittler," Pearl says. "She'd tell you that you'd never amount to anything."

Still, Pearl had a loving father. "I had nightmares," she says, "And he was the one who would get up with me."

Despite the stepmothers, Pearl grew up with her self confidence intact. Back in Towerville as a teacher, she boarded at Stump Ridge Farm with her uncle. And one night, she and her younger sister Ada ("always the pretty one") walked down the winding ridge to a Saturday night dance held upstairs from the store.

There, she eyed the accordion player, a shy, strapping 24-year-old farmer named T.J. Swiggum, nicknamed Punk, for his childhood pumpkin head.

"I saw him, and said, 'That's the man for me,' " she recalls. "He didn't drink and had nothing to do with the girls.

"I married him, and I got my life."

Beginning in the Great Depression, Punk and Pearl raised cows, tobacco and children, first at the Swiggum family farm in the valley, and then at Stump Ridge, which they bought from her uncle.

It wasn't until 1958, with the three children all but gone, that Pearl began writing as a way to make some extra money. She learned photography and sent her first feature story off to the Milwaukee Journal. It came back, rejected. The same thing happened to the next ones.

So she took her work down to Gays Mills and showed it to local newspaper editor Glenn Hager.

"Why do they send these back?" she asked, and Hager replied, "Because it isn't very good or very interesting."

And then, Pearl says with a laugh, "he gave me a job."

Hager taught her to write simply, without artifice. To get rid of adjectives, adverbs and clutter and to write only about what she knew. But, ironically, he insisted that she name her column about farm life "Spruce Hill Saga."

"He thought Stump Ridge sounded demeaning," she says.

After Hager died of a heart attack in 1968, Pearl changed the name of her column to the simple, truthful, Stump Ridge Farm. Perhaps Hager would have felt more kindly about the name if he had known its origin.

Back 100 years ago or so, says Pearl, the roads were impassable in winter and people traveled by horse-drawn sleigh over the ridges. One Saturday night, a pair of young couples were riding in a cutter to a house party when the sleigh runner hit a buried stump. They were tipped into the snow. When they arrived at the party, snow-covered and laughing, the revelers decided to call this high place Stump Ridge.

For someone who writes so evocatively about the past, Pearl has no desire to return to it.

"Who can be nostalgic over the past when the future is so wonderful?" she says.

An early sign of this attitude can be found in her Crawford County Independent columns from 1975, the year she and Punk sold the cows and got out of farming for good.

Now, Pearl loved her cows and couldn't even be in the yard the day they were sold. Two decades later, she keeps their milk records pressed between the pages of the album that holds family pictures and mementos.

But she says she "bribed" a local tavern keeper to hire her husband's band the night of the auction, so he would have something to look forward to on the first night of his adult life that he didn't need to hurry home to milk cows.

"From then on, they had a job every Saturday night," she says. "They played at places all the way to Richland Center."

A few months later, she wrote in her column that she still missed the cows.

"Barns are such lonesome places after the cows are sold," she wrote. "When I was young, living across the road from our country store, my dream was to farm. So I guess you might say that my life has been a success story. The only trouble is that success stories, to be happy ones, shouldn't have endings."

Wisconsin People

But on the facing page, opposite so that Pearl's column and the advertisement kiss each other when the paper is folded, is an announcement that "T.J. Swiggum and the Oldtimers" would be playing that Saturday night at Hillman's Bar in Gays Mills.

So Pearl lost her cows, but she got to dance instead.

This ability to see the future as a gift waiting to be unwrapped makes Pearl seem much, much younger than her years.

Sometimes readers write to her, and tell her they have no idea what to do since they've retired. She says she doesn't know how to respond.

She and Punk had fun in their last decade together, despite his failing heart. He played accordion and she danced, he fished and she, over his objections, bought him a pool table and a camper.

"That last year, we had a ball," she says. Punk had "died" in the emergency room at St. Francis Hospital in La Crosse — Pearl saw his heart monitor line go flat — but doctors brought him back. They took him off all the side effect-inducing medicines and, although his heart got weaker and weaker, Punk and Pearl spent that last year fishing and camping. Sometimes he'd play his accordion at home, just for her.

Punk died just before Christmas in 1985. The column Pearl wrote a few weeks later, an understated piece about "joining the legion of women to whom grief recurs at odd and unexpected times," was one of the only things I've ever read in a newspaper that made me cry.

She wrote about finding the joke Christmas gift Punk always gave her, a roll of stamps, hidden on the fireplace mantel.

"No, I don't know what the temperature is. He always watched the thermometer," she wrote. "I forgot to put a Christmas present out for the paper deliverer. I drove to town with my gas gauge on E.

"I start to tell him something, and he isn't there."

But grief didn't stop Pearl, at age 71, from taking up square dancing. She had taught a young man from a neighboring farm to dance when he was courting and so his new wife lent him back to Pearl when she wanted to start square dancing.

The farmer has dropped out, but Pearl still goes to her weekly dances at River Lanes in Lansing, Iowa, with a woman friend.

When she's not dancing, Pearl is pressing wildflowers to make greeting cards, whipping three dozen eggs to make a batch of homemade noodles, warring with the blue jays or working on the computer on her new book, "The Barn Came First," due out this summer.

Last year, after Boots died, worried State Journal readers wrote to her, insisting that it just wasn't safe for a woman of her age to live way out here, all by herself.

Pearl does have a worry, but not that one. Once a week, the navigationally impaired Pearl sets off for square dancing. Her route takes her around dozens of hairpin turns, down an ear-popping hill, through a herd of deer and out over the Mississippi River to Iowa.

She looks down at the flouncy skirt that shows off her still-excellent legs and the frilly pettipants beneath: "If I have a flat tire, I'm going to look ridiculous changing it dressed like this."

The Chief's Final Sacrifice
November 1994

BIG FLATS — If you read about the Aug. 29 tornado that demolished the town of Big Flats, you probably read about Frank Zernia.

You might recall Frank Zernia, as Adams County emergency government director, talking about what his county needed to recover from the devastation. Or Frank Zernia, the town of Big Flats chairman, acknowledging that 400 of the 750 residents of this poor community in the jackpine and sand country community were hurt by the tornado. Or maybe you remember Frank Zernia, the longtime fire chief of Big Flats, talking about how his fire station was flattened and his fire trucks were all but destroyed by the tornado.

What a lot of people didn't know was that Frank Zernia was dying. The night the tornado hit, he fought back the pain of cancer and got out of bed to be there one last time when his community needed him.

Last Friday, one of the Big Flats fire trucks — on furlough from the repair shop for just this purpose — led a long, long procession that carried Frank Zernia's body to the Niebull Cemetery.

It was a grateful community's way of saying goodbye — and thanks.

Zernia's death leaves a huge hole in a community that has already suffered its share of death and destruction this year.

Zernia, 59, was more than a combination of all the public positions he held over the years. For the record, he also was a sheriff's deputy, the fire chief in nearby Friendship, a deputy coroner and an Adams County supervisor.

But more importantly, he was the guy people would turn to when there was trouble. He would be the first on the scene of an accident, a big bull of a man with a roar for a voice. He'd be directing the scene at rescues and running into burning buildings to save people.

"He's going to be a hard guy to replace," said Earl Strupp, as he worked in a trailer that is the temporary office for the town of Big Flats. "The last 10 or 15 years, all he did he did for the community."

Strupp is Zernia's brother-in-law and fellow volunteer firefighter. And, with the death of the town chairman, Strupp has inherited the job of trying to get the town back to normal.

The view out the trailer window shows there is still much to be done.

Three months after the tornado, ruined irrigation rigs still lie in potato fields, their wheels pointing to the sky like the feet of dead dinosaurs. A bitter north wind snaps at the tarp covering the foundations of a home where a Big Flats couple was killed that August night. And perhaps most ominously, a 10-mile long swath of pine forest is in shambles, trees snapped off about 15 feet from the ground, dead tops dangling from the trunks. Workers paid for by a state grant have begun the job of clearing brush, but much remains to be done.

Strupp said the town is worried about next year.

"We already had one fire, but luckily it stayed on the ground," he said. "It can go up in the trees and move along faster than you can run. Next summer it's going to be a real fire hazard when all the summer people come up and start burning the debris."

The town is currently fighting fires with a ragtag collection of fire trucks loaned by other communities. Two of the trucks — one from Barneveld and another from Wautoma — were donated from communities that know what tornados can do. Of the seven Big Flats fire trucks, Strupp said, three were destroyed and the others are being repaired.

The new fire station — which Zernia designed, as he did the one in Friendship a few years ago — is being built now and should be finished by the end of the year.

"I wish he could have stayed around until it was done," Strupp said.

Zernia was born in 1935, the youngest of seven, and grew up in Milwaukee. But he moved to Big Flats soon after he graduated from Boys Tech. He worked for Adams-Columbia Electric Co-op until he was disabled in a work accident in the 1960s. From then on, he worked for his community and he worked for free.

Eileen Strupp, Earl's wife and Frank's sister, said the last year was a difficult one for her brother. He learned he had cancer and had most of his esophagus removed in April. Then Doreene, his wife of 37 years, learned that she, too, had cancer. She died this summer.

Eileen Strupp said her brother was ailing by the time the tornado hit. After she and Earl crawled out of their basement — and discovered that their roof had blown away — they set off down the sandy driveway that separated their home from Zernia's. And they found that he was already gone.

"He was already getting the command post going — and giving orders," Eileen Strupp said.

Zernia directed the rescue effort that night and, in the month that followed, the cleanup and the rebuilding of his community. He also helped people in little ways that you wouldn't know about, unless you asked.

The tornado crumbled the pressed paper shack where Anna White, 84, had made her home for the past 40 years. She said that even though it wasn't safe, she was scared to leave her home because people were saying she would have to move to a nursing home. She said Zernia came to visit her.

"He talked to me and said, 'You know I just lost my wife and I'm feeling poorly,'" White said. "He said, 'Will you do one favor for me and try to stick it out? I'd like to see you stick it out.'" And even though her tiny farm was all but destroyed, White did stick it out. Volunteers, including the Amish, came and built her a new house. She moved in three weeks ago and, for the first time in her life, has running water and indoor plumbing.

"I don't think I would be in this house without him," she said.

The call of duty overcame Zernia's illness for about a month, Eileen Strupp said.

Then the cancer spread to his brain. In his last weeks, Strupp said her brother was tortured by the nightmares of a fire chief.

"Every night he was fighting fires," she said. Zernia would pull apart the hospital tubing, frantically trying to find a hose to put out the blaze.

"He kept saying, 'Get me water! I need water!'" He feared that his hospital visitors were in danger from the flames and the smoke that only he could see. And he worried that he couldn't save them.

It was terrible, Strupp said, but it showed that Zernia's last thoughts were of helping others.

Zernia died Nov. 15. The night of Zernia's wake, Nov. 17, the Strupps were awakened at 1 a.m. by the long wail of an emergency siren. Eileen Strupp said at first she thought it was a squad car racing along Highway C in front of their home. Then they realized it was coming from Frank Zernia's official rescue truck, which was parked in their driveway. Someone, or something, had thrown the switch and set off the siren. Eileen said she thinks it was Frank, saying goodbye.

The community said goodbye to Frank Zernia at his funeral the next day. Anna White saw the procession from the window of her new house. She said she wanted to join it but was afraid the strong wind that day would have blown her small car from the road.

Enough people did join in, Eileen Strupp said, to form a line more than two miles long.

"It was like a king had passed on," she said.

The caravan of fire trucks and pickup trucks, squads and tornado-scarred cars wound past the partly built firehouse and out to the cemetery, where it stopped next to Doreene Zernia's grave.

Then, over the crackling police radio, the Adams County police dispatcher sent out Frank Zernia's last page. She announced an emergency in Big Flats, and that Frank Zernia had taken his last call and gone home.

Then, Eileen Strupp said, the minister tapped Zernia's coffin and said, "You're home, Frank."

And Strupp opened the back of her van and released 150 balloons — in the colors of red, white and blue — into the gusty November wind.

Turning to the Plain Life
November 1993

GILLINGHAM — Her white-bonneted head bent over her work, her sure fingers working a paring knife through a pile of late green beans, Leanne Beyer looks born to the plain life.

An army of newly washed canning jars waits in formation on the kitchen counter. Daughter Katelyn's home-school work hangs on the wall.

Tomorrow, Leanne will help her Mennonite sisters scrub the simple Buck Creek church in the Pine River valley of northern Richland County. There is prayer service Wednesday night and, the next day, the regular quilting gathering at the simple church, where children play outside while their mothers' thimbled fingers work roses and leaves into a quilt for a retired pastor.

Leanne's plain life is bounded by the triad of God, her family life at "Simple Gifts Farm" and church community.

But just five years ago, her life was almost unimaginably different. Leanne, now 34, and her husband, Mark, now 40, met while they were working as nurses at a detox center in Milwaukee. After they married in 1987, they found themselves in what they describe as a yuppie lifestyle: a home in suburban Waukesha, a $60,000-a-year family income and few financial worries.

But mini-vans and movies weren't enough. Both former Catholics, the Beyers searched, but couldn't find a religion that satisfied them. One Saturday, they were shopping for a church to attend the next day. They opened the Waukesha telephone book and saw the word: Mennonite.

"We thought it was something like Amish," Leanne recalled.

"We thought it might be people coming to church in horse and buggies," Mark said, "that it was something you had to be born into."

It turned out the Beyers were mostly right on the first two counts and wrong on the third. The Amish and Mennonites are both Anabaptist religions and share many of the same beliefs, especially that Jesus called his followers to live a plain life away from worldly distractions. The dress of conservative Mennonites looks similar to Amish to outsiders and some "team" Mennonites still use horses. But they also learned, at the 10-year-old Waukesha Mennonite Church, that they were welcome to join.

"It felt comfortable right away," she said. Leanne and Mark became members of the church and attended for four years. During that time, they had two daughters and bought and lovingly restored what Leanne calls her "dream house," a 15-room cream brick farmhouse south of Watertown. Eventually, they opened their "Dickens of a Place" farm (on Ebenezer Road) as a bed and breakfast for traveling Mennonites and Amish.

Leanne still remembers the time a conservative Mennonite family was visiting on a day when the peas needed to be harvested. The children cheerfully pitched in.

"The six children stood around the table and sang while they shucked peas," Leanne said. "When we saw that, we thought: That's what we want for our children."

At the same time, the Beyers had been reading the Bible and Mennonite teachings. Mark said they felt the more traditional practices of foot washing during service and modest dress were more in line with biblical teachings. When they visited the Buck Creek Church, a 30-year-old conservative Mennonite Community in northern Richland County, they felt they were coming home.

"We looked around at other churches, but we kept coming back here," said Leanne, as the October sunlight slanted in the windows of their home on a 77-acre sheep farm. "There was something about the beauty of the place and the fellowship we felt here."

In preparing for their move, Leanne began growing her hair long so she could pull it back and cover it. She began wearing the modest dress consisting of a plain, long dress, cape and dark shoes. Mark trimmed his beard in accordance with the Mennonite style and began wearing suspenders instead of the more fancy belt. They quit their jobs and put their house - which they had restored to its former splendor of birch and maple floors, a sun room and antiques — on the market.

"I left my dream house — not a lot of 33-year-old women can say that," Leanne said. "But it wasn't important anymore."

Neither was the television nor the VCR, which they sold before making the move. They said the only time they felt a twinge was when they gave up their wedding rings, because their community views jewelry as too worldly.

Around this time, their families began getting worried.

"My parents thought we were losing it," Mark said, and Leanne agreed, adding, "Both families thought we were losing it."

While the Beyers have friendly, if distant, relationships with their families, Leanne said they lost a good number of their friends over their decision to become more plain.

A half year into their new life in Richland County, they said they are still working to become more humble. Like the Amish, conservative Mennonites believe that a plain life free from distractions helps return God to the center of their lives.

"We believe you have to be separate from the world to be with God," Mark said. "We felt the pressure of living in society was too great."

But to focus on what they left behind is to miss what they have gained, Leanne said. She said they enjoy a rich community life, where their church family provides the support that their faraway biological families cannot.

Freed from the need to keep up with worldly splendors, the Beyers are learning to live on about $10,000 a year. Mark is working part-time as a nurse at Pine Valley Manor nursing home and Leanne is staying home with Katelyn, 4 1/2, and Rachel, 2 1/2.

The Beyers' life now has time and space to fill with church community life. Days begin with prayers, a Bible reading and hymn singing.

Then there is mutual aid, the shared work found in both Amish and conservative Mennonite communities. One day it might be Leanne's turn to help a new mother with cleaning and cooking. Or it could be a day to help farmer friends bring in the crop, or a women's "work day" involving canning a couple of bushels of apples, or making a quilt for people who lost their home in a fire.

The key to it all, they said, is a life where religion, praise of God and service to others is lived each day rather than talked about only on Sunday.

"We wanted a church that lived the faith," Mark said simply.

JOE MCCARTHY'S FOLLOWERS KEEP THE FAITH
May 1995

APPLETON — As they have every May for 37 years, about 30 supporters of Sen. Joseph McCarthy gathered at his grave Sunday to praise him and to talk darkly about his "murder."

The loyalists meet each year on the Sunday closest to McCarthy's death date, May 2, 1957, at St. Mary's Cemetery on the high banks of the Fox River on the south edge of Appleton. The group has dwindled some since the day of

McCarthy's funeral, when, remembers Ann Knapp, of West Allis, thousands attended.

"The crowd was tremendous," said Knapp, a short, older woman who wore an 'I back Joe McCarthy' button Sunday. "They jammed the highways coming into Appleton."

At the time of his death, McCarthy and his crusades against communism had been mostly discredited and he had been censured by the U.S. Senate. But following McCarthy's censure, 36 percent of Americans still believed he was right. Knapp remembers the priest who presided at McCarthy's funeral urging that "the torch has been dropped...who is going to pick it up?"

Knapp said the group that picked up the torch includes more than a thousand members of the Sen. Joseph R. McCarthy Educational Foundation, which sponsors the annual gathering. Sunday's group was an older one; many of its members from the same generation as McCarthy, who would be 86 if he were still alive. They included:

The Rev. Cletus Healy, who led a rosary service for McCarthy's soul in front of the grave. Healy, a Jesuit priest from Milwaukee, taught a class on communism at Marquette University during the time McCarthy was conducting his hearings. Healy said McCarthy has been vindicated, that recent files coming from the former Soviet Union show there were communists in government reporting to Moscow. As pleasure boats droned on the river below, Healy intoned the rosary and asked followers to meditate on truth: "I personally believe Joe McCarthy was a good example of the devotion we should have to truth."

Herb Stoeger, Appleton, who said he was present for McCarthy's funeral and hasn't missed a memorial service since. Stoeger set up a poster next to the grave with a photo of the late senator, a blown-up copy of McCarthy's death certificate with the cause "hepatitis, acute, cause unknown" circled, and in large letters, the words, "Who Killed McCarthy?" (The official account says he died in the Bethesda Naval hospital after alcoholism destroyed his liver.) After the service, Stoeger passed out pictures of the physically diminished senator taken a year before his death, saying they showed McCarthy was being poisoned. Asked who did it, he replied, "the anti-Christ, the U.N. (United Nations)."

Manitowoc County Posse Comitatus leader Joseph Birkenstock and a man who said he was from Posse stronghold Tigerton, Wis., and would only identify himself as "Bishop Ray." Birkenstock handed out literature blaming the Oklahoma federal building bombing on the government and promoting the health effects of ozone. "Bishop Ray," who said he was affiliated with the Christian Liberty Academy in Arlington Heights, Ill., said the current militia movement owes a homage to McCarthy, saying "these militias are a direct result of what he started; it turned out, word for word, that he was right."

Earl Denny, Brookfield, who handed out an article he wrote titled "For the Cause of World Government, Joe McCarthy had to die." In it, he says McCarthy was about to expose the conspiracy of "one world government," run by the Trilateral Commission, world bankers, the Rockefellers and others. So, these powers decided at the Bilderberger Conferences in the mid-1950s that McCarthy had to die. Denny wrote that McCarthy "died on May 2, 1957 — one day after the Soviet annual celebration of May Day. Another coincidence?"

When the McCarthyites learned that a reporter was present, they pressed in, first telling me that I was a pawn of the United Nations, then pressing me with literature.

So, to quote the late senator from Wisconsin, "I have here in my hands" evidence of a plot: to murder McCarthy, to take over the United States, to bomb the Oklahoma federal building and blame it on the right wing, and to promote one-world religion, a cause that has the pope and Hillary Clinton (at the behest of the Beast) working together.

Somewhere, Joseph McCarthy must be smiling.

GREAT-GRANDMOTHER READY TO RUN THE YUKON
September 1994

MINOCQUA — The way Helen Broomell sees it, the advantages of old-ladyhood are many.

For one, after raising six children, Broomell, 77, knew that it was curiosity she was seeing on the face of that young bear that was peering down at her.

That was a decade ago, on one of her two solo canoe trips down the Yukon River. Broomell couldn't find a dry campsite that night, so she tied her canoe to a tree and slept in it. The bear had walked out on another tree to gaze down at her while she slept. After failing to scare it off, she slowly and patiently untied her craft and drifted downstream, with the bear still watching her.

For another, the sheer amazement of seeing an old lady, alone on the river at dusk, nets her many invitations that begin, "I have an old sofa, but it sleeps good. . . ."

And then there's the fact that she will be 80 the next time she plans to go solo on the Yukon.

"I'm a good risk; I'm careful where I put my feet," she says.

Yes, after spending a day with Broomell, it's easy to drift around to her way of thinking. That it's not amazing that she's off on adventures at her age (there was that hitchhiking trip to Florida), but that everyone her age isn't off having fun.

"I like this better than any other time in my life," says Broomell, who has six great-grandchildren. "The advantages of being an old lady are tremendous."

In Broomell's case, the seeds of an active old-ladyhood were planted during a happy childhood. In 1905, 12 years before she was born, Broomell's father, Dr. John Sprague, bought 1,000 acres of cutover land on the shores of Lake Tomahawk near Minocqua. Like all of the North, the land had been left in stumps by logging at the beginning of this century. But Broomell said her father liked it because it reminded him of his boyhood in the woods of Maine.

Her father founded "Camp Minocqua" on a series of points and islands on the western shore of the lake the year he bought the land. The family, which consisted of Helen and her sister Grace, who was 11 years older, spent summers at Camp Minocqua and winters in Evanston, Ill., where their father practiced medicine.

Because her mother was in fragile health and died when she was 11, Broomell said the camp staff took up the part of her family, allowing her a childhood of great freedom in a place that she still loves. She remembers being allowed to sleep in a canoe when she wanted to and spending long hours building elaborate "fairy gardens," tiny playlands of bark and flowers with pebble steps that always wound down to the lake.

"My fairy gardens would always have something in them in the morning - a penny, a piece of candy," Broomell remembers.

It was a childhood spent sailing and canoeing and camping in the woods. As a teen-ager, she was sent to a girls camp (Camp Minocqua was for boys and Broomell had to sleep at the nearby Potawatomi Lodge) in Minnesota. Her father then married the camp director, and to this day Broomell said she doesn't know if her dad sent her there because he was interested in the camp director or if she played an unwitting cupid.

Her stepmother moved to Minocqua and opened a girls' camp, Clearwater, that still operates today.

Broomell married Jack Broomell at age 19, in 1936, and they raised six children and operated Camp Minocqua. Broomell said her husband was a drinker who would hit her when he was drunk. One reason she was still having babies in her forties (there's 20 years between her oldest and youngest children) is that she enjoyed them and she thought the little ones would keep her busy enough to ignore her husband. It didn't work. She divorced him and the booze killed him a few years later. Broomell said she has never "dwelled on the inhumane things in my life."

"I put it in a box, wrapped it up and tossed it out," she said, mimicking the

Wisconsin People

motion of tossing something overboard from her canoe.

Camp Minocqua closed in 1974, the victim, Broomell said, of a declining interest in boys camps. Parents, she said, especially fathers, seem more worried about providing outdoor experiences for their girls than their boys.

But Broomell still lives on the camp grounds, in a cabin that was a converted cookshack. Her larger house burned down in 1988, when she was off at one of her nightly Scrabble matches with her lively 91-year-old brother-in-law, Bill Cameron Sr., who lives down the shore in another former camp property.

And so her old-ladyhood seems much like her childhood. Living at camp, days spent canoeing to her "getaway" spot, a cabin on the Tomahawk River, a day's paddle from her lakeside home. Or working at the Minocqua Historical Museum, which has displays on pioneer life in the North.

And evenings spent playing competitive Scrabble with Cameron, a rivalry so longstanding that their Scrabble dictionary is held together with tape.

It seems like the perfect Northern Exposure sort of life. But as she eats breakfast in a Minocqua cafe — where friends stop to congratulate her on a recent magazine piece about her or to invite her to pick blackberries in the woods — Broomell looks out the window and frets.

"I'm always seeing truckloads of logs heading south and truckloads of concrete headed this way," she says.

Although the North Woods of Wisconsin is a place others escape to, Broomell says she feels the need to get away.

She remembers discussing this feeling with a teen-ager she met in Fort Yukon, a town so remote you can reach it only by plane or canoe.

"He said, 'I know just what you mean, the same thing is happening here,'" Broomell recalls. The last she heard, the boy and his dogs had moved upriver to get away.

It is partly to renew acquaintances with people she met on her first two trips down the river that Broomell wants to return when she's 80. The other part is simply the feeling of having a challenge and a goal ahead of her.

"I do seem to be the envy of a lot of women who wish they could do this," says Broomell, who has a license plate on her van that urges 'U CANU 2.' "It's easy. It's downhill all the way."

GREETINGS FROM WISCONSIN

ANGELS' SONG FILLS A SILENT HOME
May 1994

DICKEYVILLE — Like the house he was brought home to, newborn Scott Michael Jensen represents a new beginning.

Karen and Jeff Jensen's first four children — ages 3 to 8 — died in a house fire in the bitter cold of January 1992, while the Jensens were milking cows in the barn. Now this child of spring, born May 15, nestles into his mother's arms and coos.

"It's nice to hold him in my arms and know there's a new child in the house," said Karen, who has not forgotten the fine motherly art of rocking from foot to foot while holding a baby and talking.

Books on babies now vie for space on the coffee table with books on grieving and why bad things happen to good people. One of the presents in the bedroom is a hand-painted sign that shows four angels, Scott's name, and a saying that reads, "Angels sing when a child is born."

Karen said that in some ways Scott seems like a fifth child — because she's calm rather than nervous, as she was when her first, Jason, was born 11 years ago.

But the quiet house he was born into also makes Scott seem like a first child. After having four active children laughing, fighting and tearing around the house, Karen said she didn't think she would ever get used to the silence following the fire.

Today, signs of the four departed children are everywhere in the new house, which was built by volunteers from as far away from Milwaukee and finished just 44 days after the Jan. 17, 1992, fire.

Some signs are obvious. Pictures of Jason, 8; Jeremy, 7; Ann, 5; and Brian, 3; are on almost every wall. There are four handmade pendulum clocks ticking away in different corners of the house, each dedicated to the memory of one of the children. There are angel paintings and memory boxes and a brick shrine in the front yard that a spotlight illuminates at night.

But there are other things that only a mother or father would notice. Downstairs is an aerial photo of the farm that was taken a few months before the fire. A visitor notices the old white farmhouse that was destroyed in the fire. But Karen looks at the farm, frosted with an early snow, and sees something else. "Look here, after that snowfall you can see all the tracks the kids wore in the snow running around the yard," she said.

On the lower level is a memory room dedicated to the children. Inside are all the toys, bikes, school papers and clothes that, in a house full of living children, might be covering every surface of the house.

Wisconsin People

In this room, though, the toy tractors are lovingly displayed on shelves. The school artwork is framed. And Karen has made shadow boxes for each child, displaying special items that range from baptismal gowns to lockets.

In the one for Brian, who died the baby of the family, there's a little scrap of blanket sleeper with a teddy bear on it, part of a burned pair of pajamas someone found in a ditch near the farm weeks after the fire.

Some days, Karen said, she can't bear to go in this room. Other times, it comforts her or gives her a place to cry. She has also been comforted by rituals she keeps to remember her children.

This weekend, for Memorial Day, she'll visit the cemetery behind Holy Ghost Catholic Church to light vigil lights at each child's grave. On each birthday she brings a single fresh rose. And each year she makes up a flower arrangement with a new toy for each child's grave.

"Looking back, I don't know how we made it" through the last few years, she said. "Our family, our friends, our parish, without them I don't know . . ."

She said they waited to have another child and that she and Jeff are trying not to compare Scott to his sister and brothers, children he will know only through videotapes and pictures.

Scott's birth can't change his family's history, but Karen said, "Scott will take up a little of the emptiness."

And his birth has given his parents something that even the most loving family and friends can't — a child of their own to love.

"After he was born, they laid him on my stomach," Karen said, "And boy, did the tears ever come."

WHEELCHAIRING ALONG THE CAMPAIGN TRAIL
August 1994

WAUSAU — Einstein the political animal is the second thing you notice about Republican Jeanne Tregoning's campaign for state treasurer.

Einstein is a 4-year-old golden retriever with a honey-colored coat and a honey-sweet personality.

On Tuesday, he trotted through the Wisconsin Valley Fair, oblivious to the temptation of corn dogs and the distraction of throbbing rock music from the rides. This day Einstein was sporting his "fair" cape, bright red with a Holstein motif.

On other campaign appearances Einstein might wear his Bucky Badger cape for sporting events, his black cape with white bow tie for the symphony or his stars and stripes ensemble for parades. And for hard-core Republican events, there is his red cape with the elephants and the GOP monogram.

Even the carnies are impressed. "Wow! That's one stro-oong dog," one said, as Einstein marched on his lead ahead of Tregoning, looking for as if he was pulling her wheelchair up the midway.

The wheelchair, of course, is the first thing you notice.

The chair, which Tregoning, now 53, has used since a reckless driver smashed into the Tregonings' camper in 1972, gives this campaign a different tone from most.

If you've been to a fair or a parade or a breakfast on the farm during an election year, you've seen a politician. They're everywhere, leaping over barricades to pump your hand, thrusting literature at you. And if you watch, you'll see that they're sometimes booed in parades and sometimes people seem to be trying to wave them off.

Jeanne Tregoning can't pursue voters, so maybe that's why they're drawn to her. As they stop to pet Einstein, Tregoning will ask, in her bright, schoolteacher's voice, "May I meet you?" And, as they are taking literature about her and about Einstein from her lap and peeling off "Tregoning for Treasurer" stickers and putting them on their shirts, she is giving them a short talk about why she is best qualified for the job.

She's also using the learning techniques she once taught at UW-Platteville to drill their names and faces into her memory. This may not be the most efficient way to meet voters in a statewide race, but the people who do meet Tregoning don't forget her.

"I remember you! I remember your dog!" said a blonde woman with a bristle cut, who brings her two daughters along to meet Tregoning in front of the snow cone stand. "Remember me? I helped you get your earrings on."

Tregoning did remember. She remembered that the woman's name is Kaye and that they met months ago at the Ski Inn, where Tregoning stayed before giving a speech.

"I meet a lot of hotel and restaurant people," Tregoning said later, "because they have to help me get my earrings on and help me with my hair."

This need to ask for help is the only thing that Tregoning — a classic fiercely independent and hyper-organized oldest child — still finds difficult about using the chair.

Jeanne Brunette grew up Catholic in Green Bay, played the flute in the community band at Bay Beach and went to college at the former Wisconsin State University at Whitewater. She worked her way through college as a secretary, which is why it took her seven years before she finally earned her degree in 1965.

"I was the oldest of seven, and I ran out of money," she said, explaining her long pull for her first degree. She taught business courses at Stoughton before taking a better-paying job as a secretary at the state Capitol. There she was assigned to four legislators, including a young conservative farmer from Shullsburg named Joe Tregoning.

It wasn't love at first sight.

"I was a liberal Democrat and we argued," she said. "For a while he wondered if he would keep me." If she hadn't met Joe, she said, she might have joined the Woodstock Nation. Instead, the summer of 1969 marked her conversion to Republicanism. It was part love and part money — taxpayers' money.

"As I started looking at the issues, I could see where we had to draw the line," she said. "That year was our first billion-dollar (state) budget."

However, Joe was a factor, she admitted. "I don't think he would have even dated me if he thought I wasn't of the same mind," she said. They were married in 1971 and Jeanne opened Monroe's first health foods store, Healthways, where she sold seven-grain bread, Tiger's Milk cookies, dried fruit and nuts — and handed out Joe Tregoning for Assembly literature.

Jeanne Tregoning was an athlete. She was the top women's finisher in a marathon run between Wisconsin Dells and Portage, and played tennis and swam during her pregnancy with Josh, who was born in October 1971.

The future looked great.

"I thought we'd have a nice-sized farm," she said, "a big family, have a large garden and be involved in the community and in church."

Life has a way of surprising people. In October of 1972, the Tregonings left baby Josh at home with his grandparents and took a break from Joe's re-election campaign to go hunting for mule deer in Wyoming.

They made it as far as Minnesota. And there, on what Jeanne still remembers as "a beautiful Friday afternoon," another driver pulled out from a side road and plowed into their camper. Joe wasn't hurt, but Jeanne's neck was broken.

At first the doctors at the Mayo Clinic thought she would die. Instead, she spent the next 8 1/2 months in the hospital, some of it in a circle bed, where she would hang by rods drilled into her skull as her broken spine healed.

A Rochester, Minn., family Joe met while praying in church there volunteered to take baby Josh in, so that he could be near his mother. And while in the hospital, Jeanne began reading the Bible and developing what became a personal relationship with Jesus.

Still, it wasn't easy.

"I was angry," she remembered. "I wish that I had the Bible knowledge I have now. Then I would have understood people and had more patience." The next spring she was transferred to Madison General Hospital to be near Joe while the Legislature was in session. By June, she was ready to leave the hospital. She was paralyzed from the neck down, but has since worked to regain some use of her arms.

"The doctors told Joe he might as well put me in a nursing home because he would never find anybody to take care of me," she said.

Joe refused. And Jeanne, in her wheelchair, became a familiar face on the campaign trail with her husband. Back in those days, before motorized wheelchairs and the Ford Econoline Van with the lift, "Joe would lift me in and out of the van.

"Once he lifted me in and out nine times in a day. Joe took me everywhere."

Josh, today the student representative to the Board of Regents, learned to be responsible early. By the time he was 2, he could dial O for the operator and hold the phone to his mother's ear so she could ask the operator to dial numbers.

Tregoning said that family and "wonderful people" in Shullsburg helped keep her in her own home. They would need friends and family even more when, a little more than a year after Jeanne got out of the hospital, Joe was critically injured in a farm accident.

In the fall of 1974, he was helping his father dig post holes when his clothes became entangled in the auger. His left arm was torn off at the shoulder, his right arm broken and one leg was crushed. He would spend months in the hospital and nearly two years with his leg in a cast, in a wheelchair like his wife.

After the second accident, Jeanne said the family adopted Psalm 91, verses 10 and 11, which promise the protection of angels. Since then, the family has been accident-free.

"Faith doesn't worry," she said. "Fear and anxiety are the opposites of faith."

But in the years since, Tregoning has hardly rested on faith. She remained active in politics, earned her master's degree in education at UW-Platteville and taught at the university in various education programs from 1986 until the family moved to Madison in 1991 so Joe could take a job with the state agriculture department.

She was appointed to the state Arts Board by the Gov. Lee Dreyfus in 1979 and was reappointed by governors Tony Earl and Tommy Thompson. She chaired the board for three years and resigned finally in 1991.

Her campaign press packet is full of letters from people citing her competence and enthusiasm. There's even one from Einstein's trainer, Lynda Thorp of Janeville's Retriever Alliance to Serve and Assist People.

Thorp's letter is telling. She writes that Jeanne Tregoning not only mastered the skills of commanding a service animal like Einstein, she "offered her ability to teach others and provided excellent leadership for others to follow...she is fully capable of completing any task she sets forth to complete."

Since April, her task has been campaigning statewide for state treasurer. Before the Wausau trip, which would take her on to Green Bay and Rhinelander, she had been home for one day from a nine-day swing through northwestern Wisconsin.

Volunteers drove her and Einstein — who knows 85 commands and can turn on a light or arrange the newspaper in her lap right side up — made the swing too.

Although Einstein seems always cheerful, Tregoning jokes that the campaign is getting to her dog: "He's turning prematurely gray, maybe it's the political scene that's doing it to him."

Still, Einstein appeared ready to do another fair when he leaped from Tregoning's van in Wausau. The first person the candidate met was Don Streeter, a fair employee, who told Tregoning he was a lifelong Democrat. When the gruff old railroad man learned that this woman in the wheelchair was the candidate, he eyed her chair and said, frankly, "You're kidding."

But hours later, when Einstein and Tregoning return from working the midway and the rest of the fair, Streeter is camped out in a lawn chair, guarding the space next to Tregoning's van so she'll have room to drop the ramp that carries her back up in to the van.

Tregoning greeted him by name and he helped her find a few last people to greet. As he watched dog and candidate maneuver into the van, he shook his head and said, "Well, you got my vote."

Milwaukee's Last Socialist Mayor Tours His City
August 1995

MILWAUKEE — If you were Frank Zeidler, people would refer to you as "the last Socialist mayor of Milwaukee," and you would respectfully disagree.

Sure, the Socialist era in Milwaukee politics began before World War I and effectively ended when you left office in 1960. And, yes, we seem to be at a time when not even the president thinks government does things very well.

But you've been around long enough to see the pendulum swing. And you figure that after people see the cost and corruption created by privatizing what should be government duties, the type of big but clean government epitomized by your 12 years as mayor will look pretty good.

"Soon they (the corporations) will decide who our elected officials will be by their campaign donations," you say. "In fact, they do now."

GREETINGS FROM WISCONSIN

During your terms, you aggressively doubled the size of the city to prevent its wealth from leaking away to the suburbs. You laid the cornerstone for the Milwaukee Arena, helped start the public television station and public museum, expanded the libraries and fire stations and built unprecedented amounts of public housing (3,200 units). You and your fellow "sewer Socialists" believe government can best improve the lives of regular working people.

As you talk, giant portraits of Socialist leaders Eugene Debs and Norman Thomas look down from the walls. You are the only person in the slightly dilapidated headquarters of the Socialist Party of Wisconsin. You were once national chairman and its candidate for president in 1976.

Now, you mostly come to the office to maintain the archives.

The office shares its block of Old World Third Street with other homages to Milwaukee's Germanic heritage: Mader's restaurant; the Ambrosia Chocolate store, its factory gone to the city outskirts a few years ago; and Usinger's sausage factory, which, too, is about to move its main work out of the downtown area.

Tourists might notice that the Donges hat shop on the corner was established in 1877. Because you know interesting stories about almost every inch of this city, you mention offhandedly as we pass, "He used to supply hats to Khrushchev."

If you were Frank Zeidler, you would have lived in the same house on North Second Street since 1946. You and your wife, Agnes, raised six children there.

In the years since 1946, the city around your home has changed almost unimaginably. You note that something like 300,000 Milwaukeeans of European heritage have, in your words, "disappeared" from this part of town. They have been replaced by about 192,000 African Americans.

You grew up in Merrill Park, a neighborhood a few blocks west and south of where you live now, and your tours of the area's past and present are affectionate.

Once the German mansions along Highland Boulevard gave it the name "Sauerkraut Drive." Today, the big homes house social service agencies, and some of them have moved on because the area has become too dangerous.

You remember the families from the 1920s and '30s. You know which backyard gave birth to the world's first Harley Davidson motorcycle and in which big Sauerkraut Drive home the Davidsons used to live.

You know the present, too. Where the important Inner City ministers live and which old mainline churches have given way to Muslim and African-American Christian denominations. You're still involved with the Lutheran Social Action Conference and you know what homes your group has fixed up and which still need work. You were there when Jimmy Carter swung a hammer on a Habitat for Humanity house.

You know which blocks are bad, which are better and which resist the persistent efforts of neighborhood groups to clean them up.

"At any given time, there are 1,000 boarded-up homes in Milwaukee," you say. "The city isn't moving fast enough to replace them."

In your own yard, you have 13 kinds of trees and a bountiful vegetable garden. As you pick cherry tomatoes to treat a visitor, the squeals of neighborhood kids ring through the summer afternoon.

"This area has the highest number of children living in poverty of any census tract in the state of Wisconsin," you say.

Peaceful by day, the area changes at night, when shots ring out and police chase through the neighborhood. Your family car disappeared from in front of your home and reappeared, wrecked, in Minneapolis.

Nearly everyone asks why you stay.

"It's my neighborhood," you say. "You get to know a lot of people," you add, explaining who lives in each house. "There are a lot of decent people here, as well as a lot of troubled people."

If you were Frank Zeidler, you'd be almost 83 years old and look frail, troubled by the heart condition you've had since you were a teen-ager.

Still, you keep a schedule that could kill a younger man.

You're still working as an arbitrator in labor disputes, traveling as far away as Superior to referee between management and labor. You still serve on a boatload of committees, including one that's looking at refocusing the United Nations in its 50th year.

You're endlessly researching and writing about local history and pursuing interests as broad as model railroads and German studies. Letters and phone calls come in daily asking for your time and knowledge.

Here's your schedule on a typical Saturday:

In the morning, you have an ice cream social for the Central North Community Council, your neighborhood organization. You've been president since you left the mayor's chair in 1960.

"I'd like to leave," you say, "but it's difficult to find a replacement. People don't have the time."

In the afternoon, you're speaking at the annual picnic of the Socialist Party of Wisconsin at Kern Park, talking about the need for a stronger United Nations. At night, you're the keynote speaker at a 50th reunion at West Division High School, talking neighborhood history to a group that was still in diapers when you graduated from the same school.

You'll tell them about the neighborhood they knew, how it has changed since they left, about the problems of today and about the rocks under their feet.

Because you know history so well, you can segue from the public school that your children attended to its current use as an African-American immersion academy to the fact that it sits astride the terminal moraine of the Lake Michigan glacier.

While eating a tuna sandwich at Miss Katie's Diner, you can look out the window, past the rooftop of the Potawotami Bingo Hall, and see the Menominee River Valley as your father did, filled with the earlier native American riches of wild rice and fish.

Outside the diner's door, you can still picture Clybourn Street Avenue when the electric train to Waukesha ran along it and when the neighborhood was Irish. Back then, in the 1920s, you say your brother was nearly killed by an exploding coal hoist on Clybourn, an innocent bystander in a protracted war between labor and management.

That was back when the McNamara brothers were blowing up coal hoists," you say. "Clarence Darrow was their attorney. You could look it up in Encyclopedia Britannica."

If you were Frank Zeidler, you would be recognized nearly everywhere in the older neighborhoods of Milwaukee. At the diner, journalists, activists and Ed Garvey's sister would stop by to say hello.

One who doesn't stop at your table is state Rep. Polly Williams. That's just as well, since you don't approve of her enthusiasm for using public money to send Inner City children to private schools.

"There goes the champion of destroying the Milwaukee Public Schools," you say, as she and her group take a table, "the darling of the Wall Street Journal."

(You're boycotting the Serb Hall fish fries, too, because you don't think Milwaukee Serbs have sufficiently denounced violence in the Balkans. But that's another story.)

Back on your office block, the workers pounding and sawing away in circa 1882 Turner Hall don't know you and try to shoo you out of the construction zone inside the huge Romanesque building. But the man in the suit, bustling in the doors with the architect's renderings, lights up when he sees you.

He's R. C. Schmidt, owner of the Water Street Brewery just across the Milwaukee River, and one of the new breed of Milwaukee businesspeople interested in preserving the past, and making money at it. Inside Turner Hall, he's recreating the circa 1900 look of the old Schlitz Palm Garden.

He's eager to show you the plans and you explain a little history. (You're a life member of the Turners, of course, and a board member of the organization, which began to promote strong bodies and strong minds.)

"This was like a church to the people who belonged here," you explain to Schmidt, who is moving the old stained glass windows into new spots in the new restaurant. "So people bought windows to commemorate their families, just like in a church."

You tell him that up until the 1930s, the walls were covered with red burlap.

Down the block at the historical society, the guard knows you, too. Maybe because you're so often here doing research. Or maybe because he's seen the display on the second floor, the one about the contributions of Milwaukee's Socialists.

Your picture is there, along with those of the other Socialist mayors: Emil Seidel, mayor from 1910 to 1912, and Daniel Hoan, who ran the city from 1916 until your older brother, Carl, beat him in the 1940 election. There's C.B. Whitnall, the founder of the Milwaukee parks system, U.S. Rep. Victor Berger, and Carl Sandburg, an aide to Seidel who went on to find his voice as one of America's great poets and biographers.

"He was a great man," you say, tapping the glass covering the old photographs. "This one was a tough curmudgeon."

And, about a third, "Boy, was he stubborn."

They are, at the same time, faces of history and faces of men you knew well.

"These were fellows who had ideals for the working class," you say.

And, if you were Frank Zeidler, you would be talking about yourself.

Outdoorsman discovers an ancient world
September 1994

BARNEVELD — David Lowe has always been good at finding things. As a boy growing up in Madison, he'd come home with his pockets stuffed with the arrowheads he would find along Upper Mud Lake near where the WPS building now stands.

As a young man too restless to stay in college, he headed out to the gold fields of California in the mid-1970s. There he lived in a tent and found enough nuggets on his rented claim to support a vagabond lifestyle where every day might bring riches.

So it's not too surprising that when he set out to look for archeological riches, he found them. What's still surprising, even to people in the field, is the sheer number of Wisconsin rock art sites that Lowe has discovered in the past eight winters of searching.

When Lowe, now 39, began looking for art left by Wisconsin's prehistoric people, the state had a modest list of fewer than 20 caves or rock shelters that contained ancient paintings or carvings. Lowe, so far, has found 78 more. What's more, most of them are concentrated on the north slope of the Military

Ridge, in an area bounded by Mount Horeb on the east, Fennimore on the west and the Wisconsin River on the north.

"I think when everything is said and done, this area is going to turn out to be the most concentrated area of rock art east of the Mississippi," said Lowe, whose interest in the art has motivated him to return to school at UW-Madison, where he is working on a master's degree in anthropology. He said he hopes to bring the eastern states meeting of the American Rock Art Research Association to the area next year.

But numbers aside, what Lowe has really done is open a magical door on a parallel universe. For hidden behind this area's dairy barns, tucked away beside its highways, just a softball's throw out of its parks, Lowe has found messages from a people who used this land much differently, and for much longer.

Lowe's first "find" has so far been his biggest. Back in 1986, he was working as a crew boss at a Beloit College archeological dig at the Gottschall Rock Shelter near Highland, which is probably Wisconsin's most important rock art site.

Lowe got a tip that another cave near Barneveld might have some art. So he went and looked and discovered well-preserved art, including a carving of a six-point buck with a line coming from its heart. This heart-line symbol is common in native art and indicates the "Hole-in-the-Wall" cave may have been used for rituals to prepare for deer hunting.

"When I realized what it was, I said, 'Wow!,' " Lowe recalled. "I realized right away how important it was for Wisconsin archeology. I went out and bought a bottle of champagne. The next week I went out and found one almost as nice and bought another bottle.

"I was bit and bit hard."

State Archeologist Bob Birmingham said Lowe is part of a century-long tradition of Wisconsinites — amateurs bitten by the archeology bug — who have helped map the state's Indian mounds and discover other historical treasures.

"There's always been this tradition of amateur participation in Wisconsin archeology, but Dave Lowe's energy is just unprecedented," Birmingham said.

Lowe is a high-energy guy who, despite his work towards academic credentials, still looks like he can swing a hammer with the best of them. In fact, he's supporting his schooling — and most of his survey work — by working as a carpenter. And more than one writer has found it hard to keep up with Lowe as he clambers up hillsides, jumps tiny creeks and swings low beneath the rock ledges that shelter this old art. He looks at home with his back against one of the rock walls, out of the wind and with a view down the valley.

"When you come up here and it's snowing and sleeting and you find a dry spot to sit and enjoy nature, I think there's something in all of us that enjoys that," he said. The hunters that used these rock shelters a thousand years ago probably felt the same.

Archeologists think that native people gathered in large tribal groups in the Wisconsin River Valley during the summer, where they grew crops and fished. In winter, they split into small, nuclear-family groups and headed up these steep valleys to hunt deer and elk that grazed on the Military Ridge prairie.

So it is appropriate that Lowe does most of his survey work in the winter, when the leaves are gone and snow outlines the area's rock outcroppings. Like a true Wisconsinite, Lowe gets more energized as the temperature drops.

"I love winter, I love cold weather," said Lowe, who recently moved to rural Barneveld with his wife, Diane, to be nearer his work. (The Lowes dated at UW-Platteville and were reunited a few years ago when Diane read an article about Lowe's discoveries and contacted him.)

Over the years, Lowe has looked into more than 15,000 rock outcroppings in the 500-square-mile territory that seems to be the heart of the rock art region. He's developed a theory — based on geology and elevation — that helps him predict where he'll find the rock shelters used by generations of hunters. Beyond the 78 rock art sites, Lowe has found another 150 shelters in the area that show signs of prehistoric occupation.

But it is the art that gets the most attention. Lowe has found thunderbirds, paintings of people bent beneath their loads or holding staffs that seem to signify religious power. He's found a lot of abstract art, too: "turkey tracks" and hash marks that counted how many deer the hunters took that year.

Lowe won't speculate on what most of it means.

"I'm from a completely different culture and a thousand years removed," said Lowe, who is content to chronicle what is here and leave the interpretation for the future.

Lowe's work has its own poignancy. In the eight years he's been scouring these hills, he's seen rock art destroyed as the sandstone crumbles to dust. At one site, a landowner who wrongly thought the art would lead the government to take his land, destroyed it. Even worse, the Gottschall site — which has been featured in National Geographic and contains paintings of a 1,000-year-old Winnebago legend — was partly destroyed last winter by thieves who were trying to remove the painting.

"I felt like someone in the family died," said Lowe, who didn't discover that site but has worked there. "Every time I go back into one of my sites I just hold my breath because there could be damage."

State Archeologist Birmingham said the Gottschall mutilation and the natural crumbling of other shelters, perhaps accelerated by acid rain, has convinced him to call together a task force this fall to discuss what to do about Wisconsin's rock art. Birmingham said that because the sites are disappearing as they're being discovered, chronicling them may be the best the state can do.

"The possibilities are great for future learning, (so) our primary goal is to document the sites before they disappear," Birmingham said. "At least we will know what we lost. It's a great service David is performing."

So far, it's a service that Lowe has performed largely out of his own pocket. Last winter, a $5,000 grant from the Potawatomi Bingo and Casino of Milwaukee financed his successful search for five more sites with art. Without last year's heavy snow, Lowe thinks he could have doubled that discovery rate. But because he hasn't finished his master's degree, he doesn't qualify for most research grants. That means he's still lacking a sponsor to help pay for gas and for photographing the art before it is lost.

Still, degrees and grant money have little to do with why Lowe is out each winter walking these valleys, searching for those messages from the past.

"Even if I hadn't gone back to school, I know I would still be doing this for the rest of my life," Lowe said. "There's an urgency to this. And I know that if I don't do it, it won't get done."

A SPECIAL COUPLE ON THEIR DAY
May 1990

JEFFERSON — Both families called it a miracle.

For while all brides are beautiful and all their fathers proud, the walk Robert Fixmer took up the aisle to give his daughter, Patty, to her new husband, Ernie Gerhard, had extra meaning.

Patty, 29, and Ernie, 31, are mentally retarded. They grew up hearing that they were the children that God made special.

And for many years, being special seemed like it also meant being alone. Patty grew up watching her nine sisters and brothers go on dates, fall in love and get married and have children, knowing all the time that she was different.

Robert Fixmer chose a reading from scriptures to describe the miracle that occurred a week ago Saturday at St. Coletta's Chapel near Jefferson.

"You said: 'It is not good for a man to be alone, let us make him a partner like himself,' " Fixmer read to the family and friends assembled for the wedding.

"It is not good to be alone," he added, "but for many years, people were condemned to solitude because of their handicaps."

If her parents had listened to the experts, Patty might never have known her family.

The doctors who examined the infant Patty told Robert and Audrey Fixmer that their eighth child was brain damaged and should be put in an institution.

Audrey remembers the doctors telling them that Patty would probably die before she reached school age, and that it really wouldn't be fair to the other children because she would take so much care.

"Of course, you could take her home," Audrey remembers one doctor saying. "Some folks like to keep them, they make nice pets."

Those were fighting words. The Fixmers took Patty home to Fort Atkinson. Audrey remembers Bob working baby Patty's chubby arms and legs so she would get the idea of crawling. Her sisters and brothers joined in the project. She sat up at eight months and crawled at 11 months.

When Patty was 15 months old, her sister, Elizabeth, dressed her in a pink ruffled dress and the whole family stood in a circle around her, cheering and clapping as Patty took her first steps.

"Patty has been such a great teacher," said Elizabeth, now a Denver psychotherapist. "Things that came easily to us, she had to work at. She taught us to see with new eyes."

But there were things that no amount of work on Patty's part would change. Audrey remembers that Patty was bewitched by beauty queens and would be glued to the set during the Miss America pageant. Years later, when Patty was a teen-ager, her mother was going through her dresser when she saw something twinkling under a pile of panties. It was a rhinestone tiara fit for a beauty queen.

Audrey helped her daughter return the crown to the jewelry store.

While she was raising Patty, Audrey said she tried to be conscious of not encouraging her daughter's unrealistic fantasies. With a shudder, she recalled seeing a middle-aged retarded woman standing in line with the little children to see Santa Claus.

"I didn't want that for Patty," she said.

The teen-age years were hard for Patty, as she watched her sisters do the things she couldn't. Her sister, Gretchen, is closest to Patty in age and was her childhood companion in everything from play to having their tonsils removed. But their lives inevitably moved apart. Gretchen remembers Patty crying bitterly as she watched Gretchen getting ready to go to prom and homecoming dances.

Patty remembers being in love with Gretchen's future husband, Paul, and feeling bad that she wasn't the one he wanted to marry.

After Patty graduated from Fort Atkinson High School, she entered the job training program run by St. Coletta's, a school for the retarded run by the sisters of St. Francis. There she learned job and home management skills. Since 1983, she has lived on her own, with the help of weekly visits by a St. Coletta's social worker, and supported herself by working as a dishwasher at the Fireside restaurant.

But a job and an apartment weren't quite enough for Patty, who is not disabled in her determination.

"I asked every guy from St. Coletta's if they'd go out with me and they said no," Patty remembered. Undeterred, she set her sights on Ernie Gerhard, another St. Coletta's graduate who has worked at the Fireside for 11 years, and whom Patty thought was especially cute.

"I said 'Ernie, you have a girlfriend in the dishroom,' " Patty said. "He said, 'Who?' and I said, 'Me!' "

Ernie now says he had a crush on Patty, but was afraid to ask her out because the rules of their training program discouraged dating. After several months of dates, Patty decided they should get engaged. The easy-going Ernie agreed. Patty ordered the ring and Ernie paid for it.

When the ring arrived in the mail, Patty called Ernie and announced, "I got the ring, we're engaged!"

Their two-year engagement survived even a failed elopement. Patty said that she and Ernie were frustrated by St. Coletta's rule that forbids men and women from visiting each other's apartments. They rode their bikes to the county courthouse in Jefferson, but couldn't get married because they didn't have Ernie's birth certificate.

Audrey convinced the lovebirds that the wait for the big church wedding was worth it. That day came May 12. Patty's sisters and brothers flew in from all over the country for her special day. Her sister Gretchen, who owns a beauty shop in the Denver area, did Patty's hair. Her sister Kris made the veil and her brother Tim played guitar and sang during the ceremony.

There was a teary-eyed family on the other side of the aisle, as well. Ernie's father, the Rev. Robert Gerhard, an Episcopal priest from Ohio, helped marry the couple. His mother, Ernestine, called the wedding a miracle she never expected to see when her son graduated in the same St. Coletta's Chapel years ago. His three younger sisters were there, as well.

"I used to worry when we would leave him here that he would be lonely," Ernestine said, of the times when the Gerhards would travel from their home near Cincinnati, Ohio, to visit Ernie. "Now I don't worry because he has a family."

Patty and Ernie will not have children of their own. But Ernie is planning to adopt Patty's sassy yellow cat, Honeydew, when he moves into Patty's Fort Atkinson apartment following the wedding. The newlyweds are looking forward to a summertime honeymoon trip to the ocean with Ernie's parents.

Last Saturday, their future together stretched out in front of them as Patty made her way up the aisle on her father's arm. She was a radiant bride in white satin and lace. And when her father lifted Patty's veil to present Patty to her groom, the soft light in the chapel caught the twinkle of rhinestones in the tiara that crowned her curls.

Nell Peters Triumphs Over Life in the North
May 1995

EAGLE RIVER — If your vision of Northwoods life is from the eyes of a tourist — lazy days spent fishing on a limpid lake, nights sipping cocktails at the lakeshore supper club — Nell Peters' story is like a slap of sub-zero air.

Nell's north is peopled with drunks and crazy people, and a poverty that seems almost like another character in her new autobiography, "Nell's Story: A Woman from Eagle River." And yet Nell herself is anything but depressing. She's a hearty survivor with a rich laugh and a sense of humor about it all.

You may have encountered Nell Peters on a rainy summer day in Eagle River. She runs a perpetual garage sale to benefit disabled veterans in the garage of her home on the north edge of town. Nell Peters is a burly 63-year-old with hands rough from years of hard work. She'll tell you she had to trade in her electric typewriter for a manual one in order to write her life's story.

"My hands were too strong for those sensitive keys," she says.

Over the years, her hands have chopped cords of wood, sorted cranberries, painted houses, soldered wire, run the mangle at the local laundry and, her favorite, dripped black grease as she was elbow deep in some contraption she was fixing.

But as she talks, those strong hands might also be cradling one of her baby grandchildren as softly as she would hold a bunch of trailing arbutus dug from her beloved Northwoods.

Nell's brother, Robert Peters, published his autobiography, "Crunching Gravel," in 1993. It was favorably reviewed by the New York Times Book Review, as befitting Peters, a poet of national stature and a playwright whose plays have been produced on Broadway. The New York Times found Robert Peters book "an unsentimental look at a piece of our past."

But Robert Peters' autobiography reads like a valentine to life in the North compared with Nell's story. The difference may be that Robert Peters wrote about a life he left behind. He left the north as a teen-ager, bound for the military and the college education that would eventually lead to a job as a

University of California-Irvine literature professor.

Nell's one shot at leaving was thwarted by biology. The summer she graduated from high school, she had signed up to join the Korean War-era WACs. The night before she left town she had a 30-second fling at losing her virginity in the front seat of the local funeral director's Cadillac.

"None of the skyrockets I'd expected exploded," she wrote. Still, it was enough to send her back home, pregnant with fatherless twin boys by the end of her 18th year.

She says her brother Robert encouraged her to write her own book about her early life, and helped as co-author.

"Anyone who says writing is easy is crazy," she says. "I'd rather do 12 hours of manual labor than two hours of writing."

She agreed to the project, she wrote, on the chance she could "inspire some woman out there as lost as I was who has to struggle to putting food on the table, finding clothes for her kids and hoping for some love along the way."

Nell Peters' story begins in the Sundstein, a district of swamps, cutover land and struggling farms south of Eagle River. She was born in a January blizzard, after her father, on skis, carried her laboring mother for an hour through the woods, until they reached the cabin of her aunt Kate, where she was born.

"I guess I've always been trouble," she says, laughing, as she directs a springtime tour of the old Sundstein district.

Back amid the cedar swamps and trees, she can show you the remains of old cabins from the early part of this century, when immigrants and Indians tried to make a farming life amid the cutover. Nell lived with five siblings in an unfinished home of logs and tar paper. In the winter, she wrote, "the flimsy tar paper roof was so skinny the nails holding it to the scrap-lumber boards stuck through, collected teats of ice overnight, and then dripped in our faces as we lay in our beds, waiting for the house to warm up."

Nell can take you to the ruins of the home of the three drunken Swedish brothers: One froze to death on the porch, unable to wake his brothers, and the second died in bed, where neighbors eventually found his last brother next to the body, too sick to go for help.

Nell's memories are like that, full of detail and unflinching in their honesty. She writes of meeting her eventual husband in a tavern, her first glimpse was of a man too drunk to hold his head up.

From there, life only got tougher. She thought he would give her and her toddler boys a home. Instead, months into marriage, he labeled the twins "bastards" and sent them to live with Nell's parents.

"It broke their hearts and it broke mine," she says, explaining that one twin still won't have anything to do with her. "He told me: 'You never sat on the back of a car and watched your mom drive away.' But I told him that every time I left, I left a piece of my heart behind."

The book ends with Peters' marriage to the drunken Finn. For readers who are left wanting to know how it all turned out: She had four more kids in short order, hoping it would "mellow" her husband toward the twins, then left him and lived for awhile with the younger kids in the unheated garage her father used as a welding shop. Along the way, she discovered she was more attracted to women than to men.

"Raising four kids all by myself makes a much better story, I was the first woman Little League coach in Eagle River," says Peters, who is considering writing up the rest of her life, after her divorce. "He (the ex-husband) told me that I'd never make it without him. I said, 'You watch me.'"

Nell Peters isn't the sort of woman you should bet against. Despite the hand life dealt her, she's played it — and written about it — with gusto.

D-Day Veteran Parachutes To Remember
June 1994

STE. MERE-EGLISE, France — Every Norman village has its D-day claim to fame. Ste. Mere-Eglise, a tiny crossroads just inland from Utah Beach, is probably best known as "the village that never forgot."

Every street has memorials to the U.S. paratroopers who began falling out of the sky just after midnight June 6, 1944. There is the "Bar 6 Juin," (the 6th of June Bar) the "Auberge John Steele," (The John Steele Inn) and streets named after American heroes.

The most famous memorial is a mannequin dangling from a parachute on the church tower, depicting Steele's precarious perch as the battle for Ste. Mere-Eglise raged around him that morning long ago.

On Saturday, the beginnings of a three-day party raged on the narrow streets of this ancient town. The air was thick with the smoke of grilling sausages and, like 50 years ago, the sky overhead throbbed with aircraft as the military readied for today's celebration.

The streets were jammed with veterans — many of them paratroopers of the 82nd and 101st Airborne Divisions, coming to revisit the village they had liberated 50 years ago. By 4:30 a.m. June 6, 1944, before the troops hit Utah Beach, the American flag was flying at Ste. Mere-Eglise village hall.

Gordon King, of Merrill, was here Saturday, staying with a local family and getting ready to re-enact the jump he made so many years ago. King, who turned 70 Saturday, is one of 38 World War II paratroopers who will jump today if the weather clears. Like D-day minus one 50 years ago, Saturday brought storms and rain to the Cotentin Peninsula.

But it is supposed to clear today, just as it did the night of the invasion. The Pentagon initially opposed the veterans who wanted to jump again, but has relented in the face of French support.

"I'm not worried about the jump," King said. "It is the celebration afterwards that might kill me."

King was pictured in Thursday's International Herald-Tribune, stepping off his plane at Orly Airport and into the hands of a blond Frenchwoman who was dancing to the 1940s swing tune, "In the Mood."

The French are in the mood for a party. Flags of the Allies — especially American flags — hang from the eaves of even the most remote Norman farmhouse. On the streets of Ste. Mere-Eglise, hawkers sell D-day caps and bottles of Calvados, the local apple brandy remembered fondly by many Normandy veterans.

And every conversation, it seems, is punctuated by the sound of "crickets," the children's toys that 50 years ago saved the lives of some of today's grandfathers. These noisemakers were issued to the paratroopers, who were to use them when they landed to help locate their comrades in the dark. On Saturday, replicas of "Les clic-clacs" were hot souvenirs.

One veteran stood in the rain Saturday, beneath the flapping parachute of the John Steele mannequin, and demonstrated the cricket he remembered being issued at the noon meal on June 5.

"It was the first piece of equipment I used, a half an hour after I landed," he explained. The veteran that morning saw a shadowy figure in the hedgerow. When the shadow "clicked" back, the veteran knew not to shoot him.

This veteran is U.S. Rep. Sam Gibbons, D-Fla., who is getting a lot of attention back in the United States for replacing the embattled Dan Rostenkowski as chairman of the powerful House Ways and Means Committee. But in rainy Ste. Mere-Eglise Saturday, Gibbons drew an admiring circle of veterans who didn't recognize the congressman but who were impressed with his original cricket and parachute knife.

Gibbons, a paratrooper with the 101st, also recalled another way paratroopers identified each other in the dark that night. The first paratrooper would say, "thunderer," and the second was to respond, "welcome."

"Those were the words that would be difficult for Germans to say without an accent," Gibbons explained.

On Saturday, Gibbons also visited a French family who had sheltered him in their barn the first night of the invasion. Gibbons said they sipped champagne and reminisced. The family's 500-year-old chateau was destroyed during the battle of Normandy. But, Gibbons said, "the barn looks just the same."

Remembrance is important to King, of Merrill, too. If he is able to jump today, he'll carry in his pocket the red braids of the Fourragere of the Croix de Guerre. The award belongs to King's fellow Normandy veteran, J.J. Verga, a Milwaukee native who is in the veteran's home at King, Wis., and too ill to make the journey back here.

King chuckles at the descriptions of today's jumpers as "geriatric Geronimos." And he displays a card printed by another of today's veteran parachutists, El Harger of Munising, in Michigan's Upper Peninsula. It shows a bearded grandpa flying through the sky in a rocking chair, using his cane to pull the ripcord.

But King turns deadly serious when he explains why — after giving up parachuting in 1968 to give his wife less to worry about — he is making the jump today.

"It is a way to show our thankfulness to God and to all those men (who died in Normandy) for these wonderful 50 years," King said.

For the same reason, King is carrying the fourragere. His buddy, Robert Williams of Union, Ky., hopes to float down with a 50-year-old picture of "Jokin' Joe" Slosarczyk of Milwaukee in the pocket closest to his heart.

Like many parachutists that foggy night, Slosarczyk landed in the deep water of the river valleys the Germans had flooded. He managed to struggle out of the water. But the homing pigeons Slosarczyk had carried with him — which were to fly back to England to announce a successful landing — drowned.

His comrades say the sweet, slow-witted Slosarczyk was broken-hearted at the loss of the birds he had cared for before the invasion. A week later near Carentan, Slosarczyk inexplicably stood up, took a German bullet to the chest, and died.

Slosarczyk, Verga and King were three of a group of six Wisconsin boys who started parachute training together in the hot summer of 1942. Two of the others, Harold Lambrecht, also of Merrill, and George Siegwarth, of Wausau, died during the invasion. King said he has been searching to learn what happened "lo these many years" to the sixth, Ed Larsen, of Rhinelander.

King survived the battle of Carentan and later combat jumps into Belgium and Holland. He returned to Merrill, married, raised two daughters and lived for 42 years in a comfortable home on a steep bank of the Wisconsin River.

His basement office is filled with mementos of the yearly canoe expeditions to the Winisk River that flows into Hudson Bay. Upstairs are pictures of the grandchildren. And, even though he's retired now, he still paddles across the Wisconsin River nearly every day to pick up mail in Merrill and to run errands.

GREETINGS FROM WISCONSIN

On the homefront, King has waged battles to save two of his favorite Lincoln County trout streams from dams. He's most proud of an eleventh-hour effort in 1969 that saved the New Wood River from being dammed and turned into a reservoir.

Wolves disappeared from northern Wisconsin around the time of World War II. But in the 1970s, a pack of them returned to New Wood Valley.

"And if you think that doesn't make this old man happy, think again," said King, who enjoys backtracking wolves to see what they've been up to.

King has had, in his estimation, a wonderful life.

"In fact, to call it a wonderful life is to be trite," he said in an interview a week before he left for France.

Each day for the last 50 years, King said he has thought about the three men who never made it back to Wisconsin to raise children, fish for trout or to see the wolves return.

And every day, he gives those men thanks. If he is able to jump today, King hopes that those who watch the ceremony in the United States will give thanks, as well. After all, the people in the village that never forgot have been thanking them for 50 years.

Easter Comes to Wisconsin's Holy Land
April 1995

MOUNT CALVARY — The three bells of the Angelus ring from high atop Mount Calvary at dawn, noon and evening every day, reminding faithful Roman Catholics to pray.

The Angelus is a devotion that dates to medieval times, but here in Wisconsin's Holy Land, farmers picking rocks in the fields below are still likely to heed its call.

The Holy Land is a cluster of communities between Fond du Lac and New Holstein. Their names give this 100 square miles of farmland its title. As in medieval Europe, the Holy Land communities are named for their churches: St. Anna, St. Joe, St. Peter, St. Cloud, Mount Calvary, Marytown, Johnsburg, Charlesburg and Jericho.

This is drumlin country, where it looks like the glaciers took giant spoonfuls of dirt and scooped it into high, long hills. Between the hills is rich farmland and atop every drumlin, it seems, is a 19th century church. The towns clustered around the churches range from a handful of homes at "Little St. Joe" to villages of 500 to 600 people at St. Cloud and Mount Calvary.

Despite being located in eastern Wisconsin, the Holy Land is an area not likely to be discovered by the casual traveler. It is hidden from tourists heading north on Highway 151 by "The Ledge," the Niagara Escarpment of limestone that runs along the east shore of Lake Winnebago on its way to forming the spine of Door County. To the east, the Holy Land is cut off from Elkhart Lake and the northern Kettle Moraine by the huge wetlands of the Sheboygan River.

Perhaps this isolation helps explain why the Holy Land seems to have more in common with Wisconsin of a century ago.

As it has been since the first settlers arrived from the Rhineland in the 1840s, the Holy Land remains strongly German and strongly Catholic. Names from early census rolls are still found on farm mailboxes today. Stuffed "spanferkel," a German style pork roast, was the Holy Week special at Abler's Meat Market in Mount Calvary. Nearly every home, it seems, has a backyard shrine to the Virgin Mary to go along with the favorite front yard ornament, the statue of the little black boy fishing. (Sensitivity to other ethnic groups, apparently, has not yet seeped over the Ledge.)

The area has always been strongly conservative. Former Attorney General Don Hanaway used to say that he had to oppose abortion, since he for years represented the Holy Land in the state Senate. Rep. Al Ott, R-Forest Junction, inherited the Holy Land in the last redistricting and said he often gets letters from the area supporting vouchers for private education.

And no wonder. There are no public schools located in the Holy Land. Students from the area face bus rides to New Holstein. About half the area's students attend Catholic school instead, at St. Cloud, Johnsburg and Holy Cross in Mount Calvary.

Rev. Peter Kutch, a Capuchin priest from the St. Lawrence seminary on Mount Calvary, said that a belief in Catholic education brings young parents back into the church.

"They may not be attending church, but as soon as that first child is born, they want to know what we can do for them in the schools," said Rev. Kutch, who serves as pastor at St. Joe, St. Cloud and Holy Cross.

Teachers at the schools — which consolidated as a system 25 years ago — say that strong parental involvement makes teaching the children much easier.

When parents and teachers see each other frequently at school, at church and at family gatherings, children have a secure sense of belonging — and the sure knowledge that their misdeeds will be noted.

When music teacher Marilyn Lisowe looks out over the children singing Disney songs in preparation for the St. John the Baptist spring concert, she sees an uncanny resemblance to the children she went to school with 25 years ago at the now-closed Marytown Catholic School.

"The family resemblance is so strong," Lisowe said, that she can just see a little face and know to which family the child belongs.

Family resemblance was even stronger in Christine Birschbach's fifth grade a few years ago, when she had her younger brother, Jason, in her class. She said teaching a sibling wasn't really a problem.

"He always knew he would have to behave or I would talk to Mom," she said.

Birschbach was an example of how someone from the Holy Land can go all the way through college without leaving the area, or Catholic school. Once she finished eight grades in the Holy Land Catholic schools, she went to high school at St. Mary of the Springs, located on the Ledge just east of Fond du Lac, and to Marian College in Fond du Lac. (Boys have the option of going to the seminary at St. Lawrence.)

"I've been in Catholic school since first grade — and I'm still here," she said, with a smile.

Soon Birschbach will marry another young man from the Holy Land. People who grow up here often want to stay to raise their families, even if they're not interested in farming. The severe shortage of off-farm homes explains the sprouting of new houses on nearly every drumlin.

"The only way to stay here is to build," said Lisowe.

And people do want to stay. Edie Birschbach, who works at Marian College and is married to teacher Birschbach's cousin, said people often work in Sheboygan or Fond du Lac, but want to keep their family in the Holy Land.

"There's a wholesomeness," she said. "You can live the good life, and not have to deal with a lot of the problems."

Rev. Kutch, who returned to the Holy Land after ministering to an urban congregation in St. Paul, Minn., said the area retains a "German piety" that may be stronger than it is in other places. But things are changing, even in the Holy Land.

"At one time, church really was the center of everyone's lives; there were just the farms and the church," he said. "It's changing now, people have other affiliations."

Religion remains central, though, and Kutch has spent a busy Holy Week driving back and forth across the swamp that separates communities in the Holy Land, leading a penance service at Little St. Joe and an Easter vigil at St. Cloud, and coming to Holy Cross in Mount Calvary today to hold the Easter Mass.

His sermon, he said, will talk about Easter as the triumph of positive over negative. (In years past, the faithful of the Holy Land re-enacted the final steps of Jesus by following an outdoor Stations of the Cross up the steep side of Wisconsin's Mount Calvary.) This year they will hear Kutch remind them that what seemed so horrible on Good Friday — the killing of the Savior by a mob — results in Jesus rising from the dead on Easter.

"We live in such a world of negativism and doubts," Kutch said. "Easter is a positive. It reminds us that we can even go through death and come out OK."

It is a message that has been sounded every Easter for more than 150 years in Wisconsin's Holy Land.

FINDING ROMANCE IN WISCONSIN
February 1994

ROMANCE — Sometimes you need a little romance in your life.

And all you really have to do is pick up the telephone and dial for a little warmth. No, not one of those 900 numbers. Just the Viroqua Telephone Co. line direct to Romance.

"Rrrrrrr-omance!" a hearty voice on the other end will answer, and you know you'll have reached Kevin Wuolle one of a handful of true Romantics. If Kevin isn't too busy making sandwiches for the Romance Hardwoods' loggers down from the ridge on lunch hour, he can tell you a lot about Romance.

But really, Romance is better if you experience it for yourself.

As you drive west from Viroqua toward the Mississippi River, Highway 56 will eventually drop into a sweet valley lined with wooded bluffs. And as you get close, you might notice that the rounded hills look a little like the tops of valentines, and that there's a definitive cleavage in the hills (OK, so the trees give the cleavage a 5 o'clock shadow) and then you'll know that you're there: in the town of Harmony, in the unincorporated limits of Romance.

It may not be what you expect.

"When I tell people I live in Romance, they think it's some kind of Luuuuuv Shack," said Romance Store bartender Jean Jaynes, who still hasn't lost her Missouri twang three years after following her brand-new husband, Jeff, north to Romance.

But forget the Cupids and pink velvet settees. The Romance Store is still the pressed-tin ceiling, bread and bananas general store it always has been. You could fix a broken heart here, but only if you knew how to install and adjust the hose clamps hanging on the wall above the bar. And if you're feeling lucky, you'd be advised to try your luck at the shake-of-the-day dice cup or in the Coon Valley Sportmen's gun raffle.

Like a lot of taverns, the Romance Store now has a condom machine in the men's room, but lovers leaving together at midnight are doubly cautioned by the Pampers and Huggies display near the front door.

Once upon a time, the Romance Store also held the Romance Post Office. And, Wuolle said, it was a popular place to get letters canceled, especially on Valentine's Day. But a few decades back, the U.S. Postal Service turned Romance into Route One, Genoa, and a bit of history slipped away.

Now the only thing you can buy with the Romance name is a decidedly unromantic cap: It's blaze orange, has wooly ear flaps and doesn't go with anything in the Victoria's Secret catalog. No one is quite sure how Romance got its name, but it does appear on the oldest maps of the county. Wuolle said he's heard it has something to do with activities at a nearby gravel quarry. Author Robert Gard, in his "Romance of Wisconsin Place Names," is equally nebulous: "located between hills of beautiful forests, conducive to romance."

Today, Romance consists of two taverns — the Romance Store, which has a beer bar and a ball field, and, across Highway 56, the Romance Tavern, which has hard liquor, a dance floor and another ball field.

The true Romantics number seven: Todd Whisler, Romance's resident bachelor, whose family owns the tavern; his sister Kathy and her husband Kevin Kilmer; Wuolle, who owns the store tavern, his wife Jenny, and their son, Frank; and store tavern bartender Grace Roice, who lives in the Romance Guest Cottage.

"I love it down here," said Roice, who hails from Wyoming, "but romantically-wise, I don't think the name fits the people."

While romance is an occasional topic at both taverns, the folks down in Romance are talking about another topic with the longing tones of a lovestruck teen-ager: summer.

Once the thaw finally sends the snow heading for New Orleans, Wednesday night family softball will resume at the Romance Store ballfield. Kids, grandparents, and teens play together, 20 to a team.

"Kids get to swing until they get a hit — and so does everyone else," explained Kevin Wuolle.

Then soon enough, the folks across the road at the Romance Tavern put up the stages for their Fourth of July (and third of July) country music festival. Owner Ray Whisler has already booked Eric Nofsinger and Country Class out of La Crosse and he's doubled his camping and parking space to accommodate the 2,000 people who come to dance, drink beer, eat sweet corn and roasted pig and watch fireworks.

Then the Romance Store responds, with its annual "Rock the Romance Valley" extravaganza of rock bands, another event that draws 1,500 to 2,000 people to the valley.

GREETINGS FROM WISCONSIN

All this hot talk of sweet corn, softball, pig roasts, camping and fireworks is almost more than an amateur Romantic can bear.

But before heading back into the frigid world, get out your datebook. If Romance passed you by this Valentine's Day, you might just want to look it up yourself come summer.

Highground's Dove Takes Olive Branch to Vietnam
July 1994

NEILLSVILLE — The wind always seems to be blowing on the Highground, the Wisconsin Vietnam Veterans Memorial Park located high above the Black River valley.

The wind rattles the chimes that bear the names of every Wisconsinite killed in Vietnam. And the wind ruffles the wildflowers growing on a memorial mound built in the shape of a mourning dove, making it look like the shadow of a dove moving across this central Wisconsin hillside.

Later this year, the dove truly may take flight.

In November, a group of Wisconsin Vietnam veterans plan to go to Vietnam and work alongside Vietnamese veterans to build another dove mound. The mound will be part of a Veterans Peace and Reconciliation Park being planned on the outskirts of Hanoi, Vietnam.

The story of this link between former enemies begins in 1990 at Highground, a park that has a reputation for its healing powers.

That year, Professor Nguyen Ngoc Hung of the Hanoi Foreign Language Institute was visiting Madison. Hung, who fought in the Vietnamese Army for six years, heard about Highground and asked to visit.

Howard Sherpe, a Madison advertising company owner, and John Beaudin, a Madison attorney who died of cancer last year, took Hung to see the Highground. Sherpe and Beaudin fought in Vietnam and were active in the founding of the Highground.

Sherpe, who returned from Vietnam on the Fourth of July 27 years ago, said before he spoke to Hung, he had mixed feelings.

"I must admit that at that time, I had some deep-seated (negative) feelings about the Vietnamese," he said.

But as the three stood and gazed past the dove mound and over the pine trees to the faraway bluffs, the healing powers of Highground took over.

"We just stood on the mound and talked. (Hung) really opened up. He talked about his brother, who is one of Vietnam's 300,000 missing in action,"

84

Sherpe said. "He asked if he could say a prayer for his brother and the others who were missing."

The Americans learned that, like many of their comrades, Hung was a reluctant soldier who was drafted while a college student. He talked of losing friends, family and his girlfriend to the war.

"John Beaudin talked about how people would bring their troubles to the mound, lie down in the wings of Mother Earth and leave their problems behind," Sherpe said. "I know (Hung) really liked that idea."

The Highground meeting ended at Doc's wall, a tumbledown wall of gray and pink granite rocks in the woods near the dove mound.

"(Hung) autographed a rock to me in peace and friendship and wanted me to do the same," Sherpe recalled. "Twenty-seven years ago we had been trying to kill each other."

The Highground seems to have that kind of effect on people. Its name describes both the majestic view and the one place in battle where soldiers felt safe.

Inside the display case are letters from veterans who write about how the park has helped them.

"Without knowing why," begins one letter, "I drove in that raging midnight to the Highground. . . ."

The writer describes spending the night nestled in the protective wing of the earthen dove.

On a stormy day last month, a busload of veterans from the Veterans Administration Hospital in Tomah took a trip to the Highground as part of a therapy session.

But for veteran Mike Boehm, a Blue Mounds carpenter, healing didn't begin until he returned to Vietnam in 1992 to help build a medical clinic. The journey back to Vietnam had a powerful effect on Boehm and the veterans who went with him.

"Two of the guys said they had had nightmares for 20 years about (Vietnamese) women and children dying," Boehm said. After the 1992 trip, he said, "the nightmares went away."

Boehm said the trip gave him a chance to personally make reparations for the wrongs of war and left him wanting to go back.

So when Hung returned to Madison last year and spoke about his impressions of Highground, Boehm met with him and discussed the idea of building such a place in Vietnam.

Last December, Boehm went again to Vietnam to deliver a $3,000 check from the Madison-Indochina Support Group that will be used to begin a revolving loan fund to help small farmers near My Lai.

Boehm also met with a group of Vietnamese veterans assembled by Hung. Like Sherpe, Boehm said he was nervous about meeting the former enemy. But Boehm, a recovering alcoholic, said he was so determined to make the park project work that he drank a whiskey toast and ate cooked dog at a banquet to seal the park contract.

The Vietnamese government's forestry department donated a 10-acre rice field 10 kilometers north of Hanoi for the park. But Boehm and Sherpe said the government had little involvement with the park and that the project really was one of veterans from both countries.

The contract Boehm signed with the Vietnamese veterans promises he will raise $10,000 by the end of the summer. The money will be used to fill the low-lying field so it will be ready when the mound builders arrive in November.

One of those planning to make the trip to Vietnam is Arena artist David Giffey. Giffey, a Vietnam veteran known nationally for his icon paintings, designed the dove mound that was built at Highground in 1989.

"At that time, Howard Sherpe and I talked and fantasized about building one in Vietnam," Giffey said. "The idea was always in our minds, because the dove is the symbol of peace and reconciliation."

In designing the dove, Giffey said he drew on the traditions of the ancient mound-building Indian tribes of Wisconsin. In its heart, the Highground dove contains earth from each of Wisconsin's 72 counties, as well as objects sacred to the mound-building veterans.

Giffey, who hasn't been back to Vietnam since the war, said he had mixed feelings about making the trip, but believed it would be valuable. He said he was interested in meeting with Vietnamese artists and veterans and with "learning about a culture that my youth, ignorance and position as an enemy prevented me from learning about the first time."

Each of the men has his own reason for wanting to build a dove mound in Vietnam. For Boehm, going back allows him to continue to heal from his war experiences.

"It seems that people in this country feel hopeless and helpless about things that their government does that they don't like," Boehm said. "Something like this is an antidote — this is something we can do.

"We can't expect our government to behave in a moral way, so we've got to do it ourselves."

Giffey said he saw the park building trip as a simple gesture between two groups of people trying to understand each other.

"For some reason, this art object, this sculpture helps them do that," Giffey said of his dove design. "I'm just delighted about it."

Sherpe won't be making the trip this year because, with two children in college, he can't afford it, he said. But his heart will be with the mound builders.

Sherpe said when he and his friends began the plans for Wisconsin's Highground a decade ago, they had no idea what it would become. He has talked with veterans who were considering suicide, he said, but changed their minds after spending some quiet time at Highground.

Last year, he watched as the daughter of his late friend and fellow veteran John Beaudin danced a Native American victory dance on the dove mound before Beaudin's ashes were sprinkled there.

Highground, Sherpe said, "has become a spiritual place for veterans, a place for them to come and get healed from their spiritual wounds. (Hung) said veterans in Vietnam have some of the same problems we have here."

Sherpe said he hoped the Vietnam peace park would grow to have a similar role in that country — both for Vietnamese veterans and for visiting Americans.

"It could become a place that every veteran wants to see," Sherpe said. "And it had its roots in the Highground in Wisconsin."

MILWAUKEE'S IRISH HONOR THEIR SAINT
March 1994

MILWAUKEE — The bagpipers marching in from the spring sunshine on Seventh Street filled the gothic heights of old St. Patrick's Church on Saturday with an otherworldly buzz and wail.

The piper procession began the Shamrock Club's annual St. Patrick's Day Mass. The Mass at Seipeal Naomh Padraig, the Gaelic name for the church, is how some of the Milwaukee Irish kick off a holiday that has come, to others, to be symbolized by green beer and leering leprechauns.

The 100-year-old church still has its Celtic decorations and a glowing stained-glass depiction of Ireland's patron saint holding a shamrock in one hand and striking down a snake with his staff.

Once the church was the center for Milwaukee's Irish immigrants. But they moved on, and the neighborhood surrounding the church has been Hispanic for generations. Today, the notices for the church women's club and the schedule of church cleaners who keep it sparkling are written in Spanish.

But St. Patrick's Day week is a time for the old Gaelic tribe to gather back at its home. Saturday marked a reunion for the St. Patrick's School class of 1947.

And so, for one day, the church had a tenor in the choir loft and a sea of Irish faces in the pews. The white-haired ladies behind us — cheekbones sharp, silk scarves knotted at their throats — could have been Rose Kennedy's younger sisters. A few pews ahead, a toddler with dark red hair and rosy cheeks napped on his father's shoulder. There were handsome dark-haired men in cable knit sweaters and the ushers from the Ancient Order of Hibernians, their faces looking like they were carved from the old sod itself.

And all of us listened intently, as Father Tom Hayes told us how we came to be in this place.

"This year marks the 150th anniversary of the first major failure of the potato crop," said the Rev. Hayes, normally of County Cork, Ireland, and now studying at Marquette University. "The famine was undoubtedly the event that caused you to be born here."

And then there was a prayer for the fact that the ships that carried our starving ancestors weren't among the many that sank on their way to America.

The Rev. Hayes said the huge disaster of famine marked those, like his family, who were left behind in Ireland. There was a large stone in his family's fence that could never be moved, because it marked where an entire family had died of famine and was buried in their own field. Half of the nearby cemetery was given over to a mass, unmarked "famine grave."

"Countless died there during the years of famine," he said. "They wanted to be buried in sacred ground, (so) some died on their way to the graveyard."

And millions of others found their way to America.

"God gave us a very small island to be born on," Father Hayes told the Irish Americans, "but a whole world to live in."

He told the familiar story of how St. Patrick used the three-leaved shamrock to teach the pagan kings of Ireland about the trinity of God.

Then, there was a prayer for the newborn peace in Ireland, and mention that this is the first St. Patrick's Day in decades that will be celebrated in Northern Ireland without fear of violence.

Then, right after the talk of peace, came the playing of that most militant of Irish songs "The Wearing of the Green," which memorializes the time when the British banned even the wearing of the Irish colors.

(Beside me, my father smiles. "Ah, the Irish," he said. "Never forgive.") Then there's the announcement of the traditional Easter Mass at Marquette, commemorating the martyrs of the Easter Rebellion of 1916. (Although the British killed the Irish rebels a decade before he was born, Dad still gets agitated when he talks about it. "They murdered them! Rounded them up in the post office and just shot them!") Finally, after the hymn to St. Patrick, the pipers piped the crowd back out into the sunshine and on to a pancake breakfast.

And so started the week of St. Patrick with the Irish blessing, which begins, "May the road rise up to meet you, may the wind be always at your back," and ends, "Until we meet again, may the Lord love you and may He hold you in the palm of His hand."

Wisconsin Places

WISCONSIN'S FIRST FISH FRY DISCOVERED
May 1995

TOWN OF DUNN — Dave Barton likes to joke that this was probably the site of "Wisconsin's oldest Friday night fish fry."

Early settlers wrote of seeing Winnebago Indians standing on a rock fish trap in the Yahara River here, holding torches high and spearing spawning walleyes as the fish funneled through a 20-foot gap in the rocks. The fish weir may go back thousands of years, says Barton, a professional archaeologist and member of the Charles E. Brown Archaeological Society.

What's more, people have been using the lands along the Yahara River here going back 12,000 years, when they camped at the edge of glacial Lake Yahara, speared fish and shot fluted projectile points at mammoths and mastadons. (As Barton says, they've found "Fred Flintstone and Barney Rubble-type points" here.) While some of these rich archaeological sites have been known for decades, they're being threatened by development.

And so the archaeologists need help.

As part of Wisconsin's first Archaeology Week celebration, which will be May 14 to 20, the State Archaeologist's Office is asking interested people to sign up with the local Brown Society this spring to help survey and map the ancient sites along the Yahara River.

You'll get to tromp through fields with experienced archaeologists, like Barton. And if you're lucky, you'll experience the chill of pulling up a chipped piece of chert and learning it's a point that was fashioned 4,000 to 5,000 years ago. The site is so rich that our group, which included two 7-year-olds with sharp eyes, unearthed a half dozen pieces that will go into the collection at UW-Madison.

"I've been in archaeology for 20 years," says Barton, who by day works for a drug company, "and there are more (man-made) rocks here than anywhere I've seen."

State Archaeologist Bob Birmingham says arrowhead hunters have for years searched the area to find "some of the first tools of the first people in America." What's more, the sheer numbers of points, and the fact that the area was still being used by Indians when Europeans arrived, indicate that it has had millenia of "intensive occupation."

"People have been attracted to the land along the Yahara for 10,000 years for the same reasons we're attracted to it today," said Birmingham, who is concerned that building along the river will forever ruin the sites. "Because that area is developing rapidly, we need to at least document what's there."

Along the Yahara River, amateurs will begin work as soon as the farmers who own the fields finish their spring plowing, a ritual that for many years has brought up relics of the past. Barton says the Brown Society surveyed 18 sites last year and wants to return to three of the best.

Barton says people who work on the site will have to sign a promise to turn over important relics and to never return to the sites on their own. Even our 7-year-olds thought that turning over their points was worth the fun of finding them. Their conversations with Barton went something like this:

Kids: "Hey, look-it this!"
Barton: "That's an oops (a piece that was going to be a point, but broke)."
Kids: "Hey, look-it this!"
Barton: "That's a pretty rock."
Kids: "Hey, look-it this!"
Barton: "Hey, that's nice!"

Then out would come a flag, marking the spot. Barton would number the point, identifying it for when it arrives at the university where a graduate student is studying the site. Besides the instant gratification of the site — and looking for points is quickly addictive, the kids were splashing in the river before we noticed — Barton says novices will learn a lot about archaeology.

Because they'll help map the site, they'll learn about documenting their work. They'll also learn about settlement patterns in Dane County, going back to when the four lakes were one big one and all of Madison was still underwater.

Barton says he likes to think, as he searches, about what was important to people who camped on this land thousands of years ago. Probably the same things that we think are important today: a hot fish dinner, a knife sharp enough to cut it, and kids who stay out of the mud before dinner.

Ginseng buying brings East to North
December 1994

BROKAW — They arrive at day's end, bearing the fruit of seven years' hard labor in their arms.

Even 5-year-old Seth, the smallest member of the Olson family of Battle Lake, Minn., carries a boxful of the precious roots into the Hsu Ginseng Enterprises warehouse north of Wausau.

Inside a room smelling of pungent, bitter spice, company president and chief ginseng buyer Paul Hsu picks over the Olsons' roots, cradling them in his hand, examining them. He doesn't like what he sees in the first box.

"You murdered them," he says, making a face at the overly clean ginseng. "If

Wisconsin Places

these roots weren't so clean they'd be a lot prettier."

The roots in the biggest barrel are more to his liking — and to the tastes of the Chinese, who will spend a month's salary to buy a pound of the health-enhancing roots.

"This is just right," he says, of a load of the tawny roots that still carry the brown patina of sandy soil "See how that makes wrinkles show up? It's fashion — color is important."

The wrinkles, the color, the potency of woods-grown ginseng earn the Olsons $125 a pound for their roots. Woods-grown ginseng is midway in desirability and price between cultivated ginseng, now fetching a depressed $22 a pound, and the increasingly rare wild ginseng, which brings about $300 a pound.

The Olsons leave with assurances that they're doing well for novice growers, tips for improving the "wrinkle" and "neck" on their roots and an $8,500 check to sweeten the eight-hour drive home. They also leave Marathon County, the capital of America's ginseng area, having participated in an annual ritual of West to East trade that is centuries old. Fall is the ginseng-buying season in Marathon County, when motels like the Exel Inn in Wausau fill with buyers from Hong Kong. And when a farmer can be handed a $100,000 check without ever leaving his driveway.

It is a season driven by the annual holidays of two cultures — the deer hunting season, when farmers want to be done with the work of this demanding and fickle crop, and Chinese New Year, Jan. 31 this year, by which time the buyers want the roots groomed and packaged into gift boxes for holiday shoppers.

This cross-cultural trading of money for roots goes back to before the Europeans began settling the North. Some American Indian tribes used the "man-root" themselves as medicine. In the early 1700s, fur traders recognized the root as one the Chinese would pay big money for and sent the Iroquois Indians into the woods to collect it. Even Daniel Boone was a "shang" trader.

Sometime late in the 19th century, people began collecting seeds from the forest and trying to grow them themselves.

Ron Rambadt, executive director of the Wisconsin Ginseng Board, said the group has more or less randomly chosen 1996 as the year to celebrate a century of cultivated ginseng growing in Wisconsin.

The early pioneers, mostly German and Polish farmers located in the Marathon City area west of Wausau, had to solve the vexing problems of turning this wild plant into a cultivated crop.

And the problems were enormous: seeds that would rot rather than germinate; roots that must stay in the ground four years and thus were susceptible to all kinds of disease and frost damage; a crop that requires deep shade, back-breaking handwork and will spoil right up to the time it's dried.

And then, when the crop is finally in the barrel, the grower is left with a piece of land that's "shanged-out," land that can never again grow ginseng because some mysterious substance in the soil will kill subsequent crops.

Some of the early Marathon County growers were the Fromm brothers, four secretive sons of pioneers who began cultivating ginseng in 1904. Kathrene Pinkerton's 1948 book, "Bright with Silver," details how the Fromm boys studied the plants in the woods and duplicated their habits. They dug loam from the forest to cover the plants, built arbors to create shade and raked leaves from the woods each fall to insulate the delicate roots.

And they learned many hard and bitter lessons about ginseng. Perhaps most heartbreaking was the 1915 crop, the result of five years work and their biggest ever. Yet the huge crop, worth tens of thousands of dollars, overtaxed their new drying building.

"The boys learned the habits of mildew in a way they could never forget, learned to recognize the cold and clammy feeling of roots in which mildew was about to start, learned mildew's distinctive smell," noted Pinkerton.

"Its dank odor struck them as they entered the door; it polluted the air, clung to their clothes and skin, and always it was a dreadful reminder of defeat."

But the Fromms stuck it out, through disasters both natural and man-made. During the 1930s and 1940s, the market fell apart because of war in China. So the Fromms dried and stored their roots for better days, which eventually came.

The Fromms always worried that thieves would steal their crop (just as the brothers had swiped their first wild plants from the woods of their neighbors). In the early days, they loaded their shotguns, and climbed on top of the arbors to sleep, even in winter.

They were driven to guard a crop that was the financial key to their real dream: domesticating another mysterious species of the North Woods, the silver fox. The boys eventually built "Fort Moreland," a two-story log tower with gun holes where they could guard both their shang and their foxes.

This history of lessons learned the hard way, unstable markets and a crop more valuable than any other legal plant helped create an industry steeped in suspicion and secrecy.

This secrecy is still part of the business today. Just try asking Rambadt, of the Ginseng Board, to give the going price for this year's domesticated crop.

"The unfortunate thing is that all the deals are between growers and buyers," Rambadt said, of his inability to cite an average price. "All you hear is talk, and a lot of it is bar talk, and it's not that reliable."

But while Rambadt is reluctant to talk price — his group represents growers and buyers and one group or the other is bound to be unhappy with what he says — some farmers and buyers aren't. They say prices bottomed out in the high teens at the beginning of this buying season and rebounded to the mid-20s by the end. Most thought the market was turning around, but it's still a tough price for farmers who got up to $60 a pound in 1990, in the $40 range in the next year, in the $30 range in 1992 and down into the 20s last year.

"It used to be that buyers would be buying steak and shrimp dinners" to woo farmers to sell to them, said Dave Hitchcock, a Juneau County grower. But, in recent years, he added, "it's almost like we should be buying dinners for them."

Some of the culprits include booming Canadian production of ginseng — British Columbia went from no acres in 1982 to 1,700 today — and the problems associated with trading in China.

Widely fluctuating prices were common in the Fromm Brothers' days, too. But the recent plunge has made some normally independent growers band together. In August, they chartered a bus to Chicago to protest one of the culprits they blame for the price decline — the mixing of premium Wisconsin ginseng with the cheaper Chinese variety.

It's hard to know what the Fromms would have made of Marathon County farmers in their billed caps, marching back and forth in front of the Nam Bac Hang herb and food store in Chicago's Chinatown. They carried signs that read "Mixing Chinese White Is Not Right.

"That's the first time it (a protest) has ever happened in Chinatown," said ginseng buyer Hsu. "We had Chinese signs, too, so they could read them."

Hsu said that mixing is not only economic fraud, but could pose a health risk. American ginseng is believed to be good to restore the yin of the yang individual; it calms and cools the people suffering from stress. Chinese ginseng restores the yang: it warms the blood and stimulates.

"If you're a hyper person, you shouldn't take it," Hsu said, of the Chinese variety. Thus, followers of Chinese healing believe that mixing different types of ginseng is like mixing tranquilizers and pep pills.

Hsu joined the protest because he is not only a buyer, he's also Wisconsin's largest grower. He's been growing ginseng since the mid-'70s.

Located in the hills west of Wausau, Marathon City looks like many small rural Wisconsin towns. There are German and Polish names on the mailboxes, shrines honoring the Virgin Mary in the yards and a special section at the corner grocery store featuring casings and spices for turning deer meat into sausage. It's the kind of place where you're not surprised to see the "Hammer It Down" tavern.

But there are things you wouldn't expect to find in your typical rural Wisconsin town. The jackets from the feed mill, for example, feature a gnarled root of ginseng rather than the ubiquitous dairy cows or ears of corn. And on

GREETINGS FROM WISCONSIN

Main Street, between the bakery and Linny Lu's cafe, with its blaze orange "Welcome Hunters" sign, is the American headquarters of the Yat Chau pharmaceutical company.

While Yat Chau has been buying root in Marathon County for many years, its chief executive officer, Simon Ko, said the company became a year-round resident four years ago. Today, the warehouse is full of barrels of root, while workers create piles of root fibers that look like the world's most carefully sorted haystacks. Ko said the root fibers will be made into powder to create ginseng beer and medicines.

Yat Chau's holdings stretch from medicine companies in China, to an office in Singapore and an elegant (judging by the pictures) health food restaurant on Des Voeux Road in Hong Kong. There, Ko said, diners meet first with a doctor, who diagnoses their general condition, then orders foods (including ginseng) that will put them back in balance.

But four years ago — when record high prices of root made the company decide to grow its own — Ko turned for advice to an American, Charles Jansen. Jansen, a second generation ginseng grower, also sold Ko one of the machines he invented for weeding the raised beds.

Ko was raised in crowded Hong Kong and educated in Boston, but said he prefers the lifestyle of rural America. His oldest daughter goes to school in Marathon City, and he's keen on an old Wisconsin ritual: deer hunting. Jansen takes him hunting with him every year, and Ko's first rack of antlers lies near his desk.

Jansen said he's concerned about the low price of roots this year — it forced him to postpone buying a new pickup truck. But he said that ginseng has been good to him over the years.

From his wallet, Jansen produced a fistful of business cards from his children; among them are a doctor, a Ph.D and a passel of engineers. Ginseng, he said, put them through college. And like the Fromm brothers long ago, he's sure that ginseng will once again be good to him.

"The Chinese have been using it for thousands of years," he said. "The market is not going to go away."

Wisconsin Places

BUFFALO RETURN TO WISCONSIN RIVER VALLEY
May 1995

MUSCODA — Butting and bucking, the bison came home to the Wisconsin River Valley on Friday.

While there are other buffalo growers along the river, the four buffalo now munching grass at Ghost Eagle Ranch along the Wisconsin River symbolize a cultural rebirth of the Ho-Chunk Nation.

The tribe, formerly known as the Winnebago, is one of 34 tribes nationwide who are re-establishing buffalo herds as part of the InterTribal Bison Cooperative, an Indian group that promotes the bison as "a symbol of our strength and unity... as we bring our herd back to health, we will also bring our people back to health."

While the Ho-Chunk are the easternmost tribe with buffalo, the big creatures wandered this valley until the coming of the Europeans.

Friday's event marked a homecoming for the animals — and for the people.

Two years ago, the tribe bought 650 acres of farmland along the river and named it Ghost Eagle Ranch, because it holds Wisconsin's largest collective of effigy mounds, many of them in the shape of eagles. Tribal history says the site has long been sacred to the Ho-Chunk people.

So Friday, the tribe brought in elders from Black River Falls, Tomah and Wisconsin Dells to see their first bull buffalo released onto the land.

"It just makes my heart really happy that we were able to bring the buffalo here," tribal chairwoman JoAnn Jones said to the 60 people assembled to see the young bull. "I'm really happy that the elders could be here to see 'em come back."

Three heifers — named He-nu, We-na, and Se-ga for first, second and third daughters — had been donated by western tribes and were already there when the bull arrived.

At first, he didn't seem to want to come out of his trailer, spooked by the sight of Jones and others hanging along the fence with cameras ready. Then he ran into the enclosure, where the females sniffed him, and then chased him around a hay bale. First daughter, He-nu, butted him, but within five minutes he was trying to mount her, foreshadowing what the buffalo handlers hope will happen when he and the females mature next year.

Ritchie Brown, the tribe's bison project manager, said the bull is the first cousin of Miracle, Janesville's famous white buffalo. The money to buy the bull came from a Madison man, Nick Meiers, and others who donated to the cause.

The 19th century slaughter of more than 60 million buffalo was part of an organized attempt by U.S. troops to kill off the animals that gave Plains tribes their independence, cultural heritage and health. Meiers, who is white, said he wanted to make a gesture of reconciliation.

"A long time ago I started wanting to do something to improve relationships between Indians and whites," Meiers said. He said that meeting two Ho-Chunks, Randy Talmadge, of the tribal museum in Wisconsin Dells, and Dr. Chunk Kingswan, author of a book about the tribe, set him along the path of the buffalo.

Kingswan, he said, told him to "let your spirit be the guide." Meiers contacted dozens of like-minded people and raised $3,400 to buy animals for the bison herd.

After a prayer by elder Jessie White Rabbit, the elders moved to a neighboring property for lunch on the shady lawn of a white gingerbread farmhouse. The Shadewald farm was one of three the tribe bought to assemble Ghost Eagle Ranch. Jones said the tribe wants to turn the big old house into a halfway house for tribal parolees.

"My grandfather built this house," Frank Shadewald, who sold the land to the tribe, told the elders. "This land is sacred to us and I think it is sacred to you folks, too."

Shadewald said it gave him "shivers" to think of buffalo returning to the land. While his ancestors plowed flat many of the effigy mounds, Shadewald told a different story. He said he rose at dawn on the winter solstice and went down to the river to watch the sun rise "like a big red ball" exactly in line with the mounds.

As he talked about the accurate astronomy of the ancients, a tractor raced across a nearby field, seeding it with the prairie grass that will reclaim the farm and be the preferred food of the buffalo.

The elders talked excitedly about what traditional crops should be planted — Indian corn, squash, blueberries, apples and strawberries — and discussed coming back as a group to harvest the corn in a traditional manner this fall. Talking in traditional language and in English, they reminded each other that the Ho-Chunk were Wisconsin's first farmers.

Ritchie Brown told them, "Seven years down the road, we should have a lot of prairie grass and a lot of buffalo."

But the Ghost Eagle Ranch and its buffalo are not mere attempts to recreate a glorious past.

Tribal chairwoman Jones said that elders who are spiritual leaders have been warning of a coming dark time for the tribe, of a need to connect with the spiritual.

"The elders have been telling us that there are times coming that are going to be hard," she said, saying the ranch can provide water, food and shelter to the people if times get bad. "We are supposed to build a place like this."

LAKE MILLS LOVES ITS SLIDERS
July 1995

LAKE MILLS — If there's a glue that holds the community of Lake Mills together, it's probably made of equal parts grease and onions.

Every Friday, in the summertime, a deliciously rich fog of fat and onions hangs over Lake Mills, luring people downtown like the Pied Piper. There you'll see them standing in line on Main Street, wearing business suits and shorts, swimming suits and baseball caps. Then they'll be walking away, carrying brown paper sacks wet with grease spots. Some head over to the cool green shade of community park; others, carrying boxfulls, are going back to work to treat their co-workers to a beginning-of-the-weekend lunch.

What's in those sacks and boxes are the summer delights known officially as "famous Legion hamburgers," but known universally as sliders.

The name, say the veterans of American Legion Post 67, comes from how these hamburgers are cooked.

"It's because they slide down so nice," says Orv Scheel, a retired State Patrol officer who was tending the slider pool Friday. Sliders aren't so much cooked as poached in melted lard. And if the grease level gets too low, Scheel will unwrap another bright white brick of Oscar Mayer lard and melt it in around the cooking sliders.

This method gives rise to another theory about the name.

"That's why they call them sliders," says Ken Nadler, a retired insurance agent, "because they slide around in the grease."

The Legionnaires sell sliders only on Friday, only in the warm months from May to October. The process begins at 8 o'clock Friday mornings, when the crew arrives at the Legion Hamburger Stand, a tiny, closet-sized building wedged between a cafe and a dentist's office on Main Street of this Jefferson County community. They begin by forming 400 pounds of ground beef into 2,000 burgers.

Then there are onions to fry and grease to warm. By 11 a.m., when the stand opens, there's already a crowd outside. And it'll stay that way until the Legionnaires run out of burgers, which usually happens about 9 p.m.

All the slider profits go back to the community. Tom Rubidor, of the Legion Post, says the money supports American Legion baseball, Boy Scouts and other local charities.

Sliders are an old, old tradition in Lake Mills. Some say it goes back to a hamburger stand in the park in the 1920s. Others say it started after World War II. But whatever, sliders and summertime go hand-in-hand for everyone in town.

"I had my first one when I was too small to look over the counter," Scheel says.

And the tradition continues. Janet Bauckham was in line Friday with her two little boys, Christopher, 7, and Sam, 3. Bauckham, a Lake Mills native who now lives in Raleigh, N.C., was making sure her boys know sliders. Growing up in North Carolina, they might mistakenly pledge their loyalty to barbecues.

Unlike other homogenized hamburgers, real Lake Mills sliders are not something you can get everywhere. "I'd love to be able to take some frozen ones home," Bauckham says.

And some people do. Rubidor says that in October, when the stand is about to shut down for another cold winter, people order dozens of sliders. They freeze the burgers in one bag, the onions in another, the buns in a third. Then, in the dead of winter, they can microwave a slider and hold the aroma of summertime in their hands.

Sort of like having the Fourth of July for Christmas.

They gather in Wyoming Valley to sing hymns
June 1993

SPRING GREEN — Every first Sunday in summer they come, some driving more than an hour to the little white church in the deep green valley.

They gather in this simple sanctuary, its worn wood dappled with mellow color when the afternoon sunlight seeps through the old stained glass. And their voices, young and old, professional and plain, twine and rise together to caress the hymns that were old when this 91-year-old church was built.

They begin with "Nearer my God to Thee," build through "The 23rd Psalm," "Faith of Our Fathers," "Amazing Grace" and "Spirit of God Descend Upon My Heart," and soon the old floorboards themselves are alive, humming and vibrating with the sweet sound of five dozen voices raised in praise.

"I've been coming for more than a year and I'm still amazed by the acoustics of this church," whispered the Rev. George Anderson, as he thumbed through the First Methodist Hymnal. "You can feel it right down to your toes when you sing."

Rev. Anderson's retirement job is serving Wyoming Valley Methodist

Church, as well as churches in Avoca and Gotham. But on Sunday afternoons during the Hymn Sing, he's strictly a back-pew participant. In the 14 years since the ecumenical sings began, they have evolved into a religious version of top 40 radio: more songs, less talk, and golden oldies by request.

At the last Hymn Sing, the singers set aside the hymnal for well-thumbed paperback, "Spiritual Life Songs," which contains hundreds of old favorite hymns. Soon the voices are booming the refrain:

I am living on the mountain Underneath a cloudless sky
I am drinking at the fountain That never shall run dry
O Yes! I'm feasting on the manna from a bountiful supply
For I am dwelling in Beulah land.

For some, the monthly Hymn Sings are a chance to dwell for a few hours in an earthly version of Beulah Land. After two hours of making traditional music in the kind of place Norman Rockwell used to paint, one almost expects to see horses and carriages parked outside.

For others, it is another chance to worship. Paul Ranum of Arena, known to Hymn Sing regulars as "the singing farmer," usually offers up a solo in his rich baritone.

"I enjoy being able to go out and praise the Lord," said Ranum. "I feel that it is a ministry He has given me. Other people pray. I try to sing."

But even people who have less than celestial voices can feel right at home. In fact, Hymn Sings are a godsend to those who love to sing but can't.

"There are so many strong voices that you can blend right in," said Brad Glass, a Dodgeville attorney who checked out a Hymn Sing at his neighborhood church and "got hooked."

That happens. Margi Jones has been driving from Madison for nearly every Hymn Sing since she first came to the little white church in 1986.

"I come because I like to sing a lot without the formality of a church service," Jones said. "It's also neat that people of all denominations come together to sing and all the things they argue about are irrelevant."

For Jerome Hickcox, Janesville, the Hymn Sings are a chance to visit the valley where his ancestors once lived and an opportunity to sing those old songs that rarely make it into church services these days.

"I love the old hymns," said Hickcox, who is studying to be a Baptist minister. "I'm a gospel singer and the old hymns really appeal to me."

The first hour of the Hymn Sing is all requests. People call out hymn numbers, some asking for the same hymns month after month.

"When a song is requested, I'm beginning to know who requests it," said Janet Suhr, the church treasurer and a Hymn Sing regular.

Some give reasons for their choices, like the woman at the June sing who said that when she was learning to play the piano, "My Mother's Bible" was the only song her grandfather would sing with her.

Others give their hymn numbers and leave everyone to wonder: Did a homesick Norwegian choose Sibelius' "This is My Song?" Was it a sailor's mother who asked for "Eternal Father, Strong to Save," with its refrain, "Oh hear us when we cry to thee for those in peril on the sea?"

Do those songs speak to old memories or the need for comfort today?

Rev. Anderson said he only knows this: "They usually go right for the golden oldies that we don't sing much anymore. It's like there is a real longing for them."

Chippewa Fighting Island Battle Again
April 1994

LAC DU FLAMBEAU — The first battle of Strawberry Island was fought almost 300 years ago with axes and French rifles. When it was done, the Chippewa had banished the Sioux from the wild rice lakes of Northern Wisconsin.

The second battle of Strawberry Island is being fought this year in Madison with checkbooks and lawyers.

If the Chippewa prevail this time, they'll win the right to buy back an island at the heart of their reservation and culture — a place they won't visit out of respect for the spirits there.

If they lose, the island's owner, Aspen, Colo., developer Walter Mills, has said he'll carve the island into 16 lots for exclusive vacation homes.

The battle for Strawberry Island has drawn the attention of the State Historical Society of Wisconsin, which in March ranked the island as the state's second most endangered historic site. The Nature Conservancy has also pledged to help the tribe buy back the island. But the tribe will eventually have to repay the loan.

Pat Hrabik runs the tribe's real estate office from a cluttered room in what was the boys' dormitory of the circa 1894 boarding school in Lac du Flambeau. She and other tribal members — many of whom thought the tribe did own the island — view the negotiations with a wry dismay.

"It really sticks in the craw of the tribe that we're going to have to buy it back," Hrabik said, adding that at times during earlier negotiations, Mills' price had approached $1 million. Mills declined to be interviewed for this story, citing the ongoing negotiations.

On the wall of Hrabik's office is a map of the Lac du Flambeau reservation, in Vilas County about 10 miles northwest of Minocqua. The map is a checkerboard of red, green and white squares that show land ownership patterns on the reservation. The reservation's big lakes — such as Fence and Crawling Stone — are ringed almost entirely in red.

"Red is allotment land sold to non-Indians; you'll notice they have all the lakeshore, the most valuable land," Hrabik said. "We don't have any access at all to White Sand Lake."

The story of how the Chippewa lost Strawberry Island begins with a little boy who died in 1904. It echoes how Indian people lost some of their most valuable land.

Strawberry Island, a 26-acre chunk of pine and hardwoods, sits in Flambeau lake, just off the point of a campground and visible from Lac du Flambeau's main drag, Highway 47. It shares Flambeau Lake with Medicine Rock, a place where followers of the traditional Ojibwa religion offer tobacco, and with the Bear River Pow-Wow grounds, a sacred gathering spot for Chippewa from across the North.

Indian people have used the island since 200 years before the birth of Christ, according to archaeological work done by Beloit College professor Robert Salzer. During some preliminary digs in 1966, Salzer found evidence of significant settlements between 700 and 1400, as well as a late 19th century occupation.

The battle between the Chippewa and the Sioux is harder to document. Salzer said arrowheads found on the island could have been used for fighting or hunting. But the battle is still part of the oral tradition of both tribes. The Chippewa say that poison ivy that covers the island is all that remains of their traditional enemy.

In 1976, Salzer wrote to Anthony Earl, then secretary of the Department of Natural Resources, to urge protection of the island.

"No other single archaeological site in northern Wisconsin is as important as is Strawberry Island," Salzer wrote. While the site was later listed with the National Register of Historic Sites, that designation alone can't stop development.

The treaty of 1854 between the Chippewa nation and the United States allowed the Lac du Flambeau band to keep about 36 square acres of lake and woodland centered around Flambeau Lake. But the Dawes Allotment Act of 1887 opened the door to a piecemeal land rush on every reservation in the country.

The act sought to help Indians by assigning them pieces of the reservation to own as private property.

Carol Brown Biermeier, the attorney who represents the tribe in negotiations with developer Mills, said the allotment act led to the loss of more than a quarter of the Lac du Flambeau reservation, including most of its prime lakeshore.

"They had good intentions — let's assimilate these people," said Brown Biermeier, who grew up in Lac du Flambeau and now heads the Indian Law Center of the UW Law School. "But a major problem in Lac du Flambeau was that most of it was under water (in marshes and swamps)." The Chippewa who tried to make a go of farming often found that they owned a swamp. Others had their allotments split between tiny parcels of land scattered across the reservation. And, since the Chippewa traditionally spent the year moving between seasonal hunting and fishing camps, some might not have understood the idea of owning a fixed piece of land and the rights that went with ownership.

The yellowing pages of the allotment book in Hrabik's office show that Strawberry Island was assigned to a little boy named Harold Whitefeather. Harold, the son of Na-wa-kwe-gi-ji-go-kwe and John Whitefeather, died in 1904 at age 5.

In 1910, his parents sold the island to non-Indians Charles and Edwin Mills for $2,105.

"It was a fair price," Brown Biermeier said. "Especially considering that a lot of land was sold for whiskey."

But other parts of the transaction are less straightforward. The Dawes Act contained restrictions designed to prevent Indians from being cheated. Indians needed to be proven competent by the Bureau of Indian Affairs before they could sell their land — a farcical process that Brown Biermeier described as involving "boilerplate" answers to such questions as "Do you use intoxicants?"

Tellingly, she said, full-blood Indians had to prove their competency to sell land, while mixed race people were assumed to be competent.

"I find that very offensive," she said.

Documents show that while the sale took place in 1910, Harold's parents weren't judged competent until 1920. And it wasn't until 1944 that the parents were officially determined to be Harold's heirs.

The Mills family has left the island largely untouched.

The Chippewa have also mostly stayed away. In Lac du Flambeau — a place where it seems that everyone goes fishing — it is hard to find anyone who has been to the island.

Like a lot of Flambeau children, Brown Biermeier was warned — by her grandfather, a member of the drum society who practiced the traditional ways - not to go out to the island.

Her brother disobeyed and tried to camp there with some friends. Brown Biermeier said they were frightened away in the middle of the night by dancing lights they saw in the woods.

Other tribal members told similar stories during a public hearing held in Lac du Flambeau in February.

"We don't go to the island," Brown Biermeier said. "It is a place of respect, a place for the spirits."

And it stayed that way for many years. Walter Mills inherited the island in the 1960s. In the mid-1970s, he won Vilas County zoning approval for subdividing the island into 16 lots. Around the same time he began offering the tribe the chance to buy the island.

But the two sides never came close to agreement, Hrabik said, and negotiations stalled.

The latest round was launched last fall, when tribal members noticed workers marking and cutting trees on the island. Thinking that it still belonged to the Chippewa, the tribal members reported the workers to the tribal office.

Mills reportedly told several people that he was ready to move heavy equipment onto the island to begin construction this spring. Reached by telephone this week, he declined comment, saying, "intentions change day to day."

Richard Lehmann, a Madison attorney who is negotiating for Mills, also declined to answer questions, saying, "We're trying to get a lot of people to the table with their checkbooks."

While both sides are optimistic about reaching agreement, their views about value of the island demonstrate the clash of cultures.

Lehmann said, "We're trying to bridge a gap between what (Mills) is entitled to, for years of paying property taxes and not developing it, and what the tribe is able to come up with."

But Brown Biermeier said that the worth of the island can't be measured in economic terms.

"It has more significance," she said. "It's an ethereal place, a place out of our history."

A group of young Lac du Flambeau men who paused to check out the melting ice on Flambeau Lake earlier this month had a different angle on the battle over Strawberry Island. They laughed at the idea that anyone would build a vacation home on a place possessed by spirits of the past.

"You would be haunted over there," Augie Allen said, comparing it to a horror movie classic. "It would be like 'The Shining.'"

Wisconsin Seasons

THE SMELLS OF WISCONSIN
Winter 1995

*I smell Wisconsin thawing, the varied aromas
I smell those of paper mills, cheese plants and bakeries,
each sending its own scent, blithe and strong.
The summer smells that belong to the warmth,
And in the winter thaw, the smells of the farm, robust.
So freely smell with open nostrils their strong, odiferous smells.*

With deep apologies to Walt Whitman, I believe you can smell Wisconsin thawing. I believe that some time soon, all those scents stored up over the cold winter will begin to thaw. And as the ice that bound them melts away, the smells stored up over a long winter will be unleashed on the state.

Maybe this isn't scientific. But how do you explain the fact that during a cold snap the only things you can smell are wood smoke and bus exhaust, and that after the thaw you can smell it all?

But if you can smell Wisconsin thawing, what exactly does it smell like?

Well, that, as Whitman knew, depends on where you're sniffing.

When a friend of mine moved to Appleton to work at Lawrence University, she asked someone about that puzzling, permeating smell.

105

What smell?

That smell, the cloud that hangs over the lower Fox Valley, home to the world's heaviest concentration of paper mills.

If you're not used to them, paper mill towns like Appleton, Kaukauna and Mosinee on the Wisconsin River smell like sulfur. They seem suffused with an irritating cloud that coats the back of your throat like post nasal drip from a terrible sinus infection. But the people who live there smell it differently.

"That," my friend was told, "is the smell of money."

Money smells different around Wisconsin. And, like the paper mills, one person's bad smell is another's whiff of fortune.

You can go to Fort Atkinson, for example, and ask people if they've noticed that their town smells like onions from the Moore's plant where they make onion rings.

Yeah, they'll say, they've smelled the onions. But have you been up the road to Jefferson?, they'll ask. Jefferson smells like dog food.

Five miles up the road in rival Jefferson, you might find a person or two who will allow that, yes, they have noticed an aroma on certain days from the big Friskies plant that sits next to the Main Street bridge over the Rock River. But, they'll quickly add, "Go over to Waterloo. The whole town smells like pickles!"

And in Waterloo, it's easy to find the Van Holten pickle factory on the west edge of town. There's a certain tang in the air, a nip of vinegar, a hint of dill near those big green vats. On days when they're running the koshers, you'll smell garlic; on spicy pickle days, an eye-watering tickle of red pepper.

Yes, people in Waterloo will acknowledge, sometimes you can smell the pickles. But pickles smell good. If you want to smell something bad, go down Highway 19 to Marshall. Go on a hot day. And when you pass the rendering plant, roll down the window and drive real slow.

Even on a frosty winter day, a certain je ne sais quoi hangs over the east end of Marshall. This is home to the Marshall Dead Stock Removal Co. You may have seen their trucks on the highway, with the signs that read "Your local used cow dealer." The Marshall rendering plant is where used cows go to become more useful.

Of course, cows contribute to the smells of Wisconsin long before they're used up, creating an essential component of Wisconsin's dairy air.

The wafting scent of thawing manure is one of the sure signs that early spring is here. And the manure of each animal has its own distinct fragrance. There is the ammonia scent of chicken manure from Creekwood Farms near Lake Mills, the sour milky smell of Underhill Veal near Spring Green.

And be assured that for every kind of manure, there's a farmer who thinks it doesn't smell that bad.

State Rep. DuWayne Johnsrud, R-Eastman, is a rare kind of politician, one willing to take a stand on a controversial issue. And, in front of God and Wisconsin's dairy farmers, Johnsrud is willing to say, for the record, that pig manure smells better than cow manure.

"It does," he says. "Cow manure is nasty."

Now, this is no idle opinion. In his new role as chair of the Assembly Natural Resources Committee, Johnsrud will be Wisconsin's King of Manure as his committee oversees the controversial new animal waste handling rules making their way through the Legislature.

Johnsrud speaks ominously of an ill-designed, 800-foot-long liquid manure pit near Viroqua and an earthen dam in Richland County that is holding back 6 million gallons of pig manure as "mini-Chernobyls, ready for manure meltdown."

And Johnsrud, a hog and beef farmer from Crawford County, knows manure on an up-close-and-personal basis, as many of his colleagues can attest.

Back in 1984, when he was first elected to the Assembly, Johnsrud used to make the long drive to Madison in the same truck he'd use to haul hogs.

"It would kind of permeate my suits," he said of the smell he doesn't think is half bad. "And I would sit in these hot, stuffy hearing rooms. And I'd notice people moving away from me. It took me a long time to catch on."

Johnsrud bought a car. But he has one final thought for his urban colleagues.

"To me, the cities smell worse than the countryside," he says. "You tell people from the city, 'Boy, it stinks here,' and they don't know what you mean. I guess it all depends on what your snoot is used to."

But some smells, many of them the smells of beloved foods, seem universally pleasing.

What driver hasn't slowed down on East Washington Avenue in Madison to prolong the experience of driving through that cloud of heavenly, yeasty, baking bread that floats out of the Gardner Bakery?

And who can keep the windows up on a summer day when driving through the mint farms near Cottage Grove?

Wisconsin's North Woods has its own piney freshness, the sand country of central Wisconsin a sort of woodsy, spicy oak smell that retired Wisconsin State Journal columnist Steve Hopkins says "just smells relaxing." And in the pines and oaks are tens of thousands of summer cottages, each with its personal musty mixture of pine cones and mothballs that welcomes returning vacationers every summer with its comforting sameness.

Some of Wisconsin's smells are seasonal. The smoky fire of the sugarbush that transforms spring's sap into pancake syrup.

The stench of mayflies in La Crosse and lake flies in Oshkosh, after they breed, live for a day, and die away in May. The metallic, poisonous smell of rootworm insecticide that floats over rural Wisconsin at corn planting time. The sweet May scent of the pink and white apple orchards that floats above the Kickapoo River Valley like a dream.

In late May, there is the smell of new hay, beginning its winey ferment inside the blue silos that dot Wisconsin's countryside. In July, on some of the Apostle Islands, there is the perfume of wild strawberries and blueberries ripening together in a tangled carpet. And in August, near the Madison lakes, the fishy, green, weedy smell that leads people to ask, "Can you smell the lake?"

And in fall, there is smoke again, from the fires of leaves and scarecrows burning.

Some of Wisconsin's smells live only in memory. No child who grew up in Milwaukee in the 1960s can forget alewives, those invading fish from the sea that grew and died in profusion, and rotted in reeking piles along Lake Michigan, giving off a smell that drove lake dwellers inland in summer. Now, the alewives have all but disappeared, replaced by a new foreign menace, the non-scented zebra mussel.

Another lost Milwaukee smell is more likely to be mourned. For decades, the Ambrosia Chocolate plant bathed downtown Milwaukee with the wonderful smell of melting chocolate. The chocolate aroma was especially strong down at the Milwaukee County Courthouse, where it cradled criminal and cop alike in its warm, cocoa embrace.

But, alas, three years ago, Ambrosia Chocolate built a new plant near Menomonee Falls, just north of where they build Harley-Davidsons. If you can find the anonymous industrial building squatting in the shadows of Highway 45, you may be disappointed. New air pollution control technology seems to have put the lid on one of Milwaukee's most treasured smells. Only if you drive into the parking lot, roll down your car window and inhale deeply, might you catch the faintest scent of toasting cocoa beans.

But take heart, one of Milwaukee's landmark smells hasn't melted. The Red Star Yeast plant is still fermenting away, sending up its yeasty steam plume from beneath the 27th Street viaduct. For decades, Red Star has welcomed visitors to downtown Milwaukee with a smell like a beer-belched greeting from a big-bellied friend.

If there is a holy trinity of Wisconsin foods, they would have to be the beer, the bratwurst and the cheese.

You can smell the big breweries in La Crosse and Milwaukee, but it's nice to get up close to beer making, the way visitors can at smaller breweries like Gray's Brewing Company in Janesville.

If you climb the ladder along one of the huge stainless steel wort vats, you can inhale the beginnings of Gray's Honey Ale. The warm steam is full of cooking honey and the caramel smell of malted barley, cut by the bitter astringency of hops added just at the end. Only when the ale reaches the fermenters, and the yeast is added, does it begin to smell like beer. Brewmaster Keith Wayne will tap a blob of creamy yeast foam off the bottom of the tank, and it smells good enough to eat. Or to drink.

The best place to smell bratwurst is not where they're made, but where they're grilled. And that would be beneath the spicy charcoal haze that hangs over Camp Randall on football Saturdays, over Lambeau Field on Packer Sundays and over County Stadium any time the Brewers play and their fans throw tailgate parties.

Wisconsin's cheese factories smell a lot like breweries — soapy and full of the chlorine-based cleaners that keep them sanitary. But cheese factories like Prima Kase near Monticello, which makes big wheels of award-winning Swiss in copper kettles, have another smell. It's a sweet, milky aroma, like the burp of a clean, sleepy baby.

If you want to smell serious cheese, you have to go a few hills and valleys to the south, into the heart of Green County's cheese country. There you'll find Chalet Cheese Cooperative, the only Limburger plant in the United States. And deep inside the factory, you'll find the cure room. There, cheesemakers "smear" the mild white blocks of fresh cheese with a secret bacterial culture that develops the unique texture, flavor and aroma of Limburger.

"Some people will come in here and say it smells terrible," says Myron Olson, the plant's congenial owner, "But other people will say, 'It smells like Limburger.'"

Now Myron can tell more Limburger jokes than you can, and he knows that some people buy his odorous cheese for a joke, to put on the engine manifolds of the honeymoon cars of newlyweds. But he turns serious when he discusses the situation that America has come to. In the 1930s, when there were many fewer of us, Americans ate 11 million pounds of Limburger.

"They ate it on their toast in the morning, in a sandwich with onion at lunch, and sliced it over their potatoes for dinner," Olson says. Now, though, Americans prefer milder, younger cheese and the Chalet plant is the last one left, producing less than a million pounds of Limburger a year. Olson thinks he knows why.

"Turn on your television set, and how many commercials do you see for deodorant, soap and mouthwash?" Olson says. "Everything is supposed to be clean and sterile. You're not supposed to smell like anything."

While it would probably be right and just to celebrate the smells of the thaw with a Limburger sandwich, I'll leave you with a less controversial Wisconsin smell — the aroma of a Friday night fish fry.

The fish fry — with its beginnings in Catholic and Orthodox abstinence from meat on Fridays — is the quintessential Wisconsin meal. Sure, you're more likely to see lake perch and potato pancakes in eastern Wisconsin, cod and french fries farther from Lake Michigan. But all of Wisconsin is united by a greasy ritual unknown in other parts of the country, the rite of "going out for fish" on a Friday night.

If Wisconsin is the World Capital of the Friday night fish fry, then Serb Hall in Milwaukee serves the mother of all fish fries. During Lent, which is approaching as surely as the thaw, chef Gus Anthonasin will serve more than 2,400 pounds of fish, 1,050 pounds of french fries, 400 pounds of homemade coleslaw and a mountain of buttered rye bread on a single Friday night.

More than 1,000 people crowd into Serb Hall on a Friday night. And, Anthonasin says, another 800 more will get their fish fries by going through the drive-through window. When they pull out of the lot, across from the copper-green domes of St. Sava's Serbian Orthodox Cathedral, they'll be carrying home brown paper bags full of fish fry.

And when they unroll the bags at home, they'll breathe in the smells of fish and grease, potatoes and cabbage, rye bread and butter — the smells of Wisconsin.

AND MORE FAVORITE SMELLS
Winter 1995

Just back from vacation in California, I'm still carrying the smells of San Francisco in my coat pocket.

When I rub together the eucalyptus buds that my children gathered during our visit, they give off a clean, menthol, Vicks Vap-O-Rub smell that conjures hikes along misty paths in the Presidio and Golden Gate Park.

Our San Francisco friends and relatives had moved to new homes since our last visit, but in each case had re-created the pleasantly recognizable smells of their old places. Our noses told us who was who.

We returned last week to the familiar smell of our own home — made more familiar by the milk we forgot in the refrigerator — and to a pile of letters sent by readers nominating their favorite (and least favorite) smells of Wisconsin.

It doesn't take a psychologist to notice that we Wisconsinites are very, very anxious for spring.

The overwhelmingly most popular smell of Wisconsin was that of fresh mown hay.

Some readers went further, and nominated all the smells of spring as their favorites.

"There is nothing like the fresh, clean smell of a Wisconsin spring after the cold, dank winter," Margaret C. Meade of Ridgeway wrote.

"The smell of the pure snow melt water as it roars, racing down the small streams in the country that were, only a few weeks before, snow-filled, tiny, spring-fed streams. The air is pungent, filled with the scent of the wild plums, with their white, delicate flowers."

Shelley M. Zimmerman of Monroe agreed, writing, "I enjoy the smell of first mowed grass. It makes me appreciate the life and newness this time offers. In May while walking, I love the fresh fragrance of lilacs.

"Finally, I enjoy the traditional hanging of the clothes outside. What a heavenly scent!"

Some readers nominated a favorite spring spot.

For Bill R. Laurence of Madison it is a sandbar in the middle of the Lower Wisconsin River.

"Smelling the damp sandbars while canoeing on the Lower Wisconsin River in the spring after their recent cleansing by the snow melts from northern Wisconsin," he wrote, of his favorite smell. "This mixed with the blooming of marshland grasses, wild flowers and the budding of the lowland trees provides a pleasurable, relaxing smell. You have to experience it to appreciate it!"

For Anna Zettle of Monroe, there's no better place than the farm in spring.

"There is nothing that can compare with the smell of freshly turned-by-the-plow dirt in the spring. By the end of March, you can smell the fresh dirt smell, but it takes some working of the soil to really give my sense of smell a rush. Fresh mown hay is a close second for olfactory delight."

Zettle, a farm wife, also adds a farm smell that makes her "physically ill." The smell of Eptam, an herbicide applied to the dirt when alfalfa (which will become the sweet hay of May) is planted.

The smell of dirt appealed to Kris Wheelock when he was a second-grader in Richland Center. Kris buried her nose in different kinds of it while researching a science report for school. Her mom, Jeanne Wheelock, saved this "treasure" for 14 years and sent along a copy of it.

"Wood soil is kind of smelly, not really, though," Kris wrote, in painstaking 7-year-old printing. "Swamp soil is the stinkiest. It has grass in it. Tobacco soil stinks quite a lot. Road cut does not stink. I tried it yesterday."

Robert and Rita Harvey of Sun Prairie agreed about hay and add another smell, "our fresh air after a storm."

They added that they appreciate Wisconsin's air after returning from Phoenix, which had carbon monoxide alerts and a ban on burning in fireplaces.

Freshly mown grass, the city cousin of hay, received several votes. But for golfer John Stamler of Madison, it has to be a certain kind of grass.

"On an early summer morn, with clubs at hand, following the mowers on the golf course and inhaling the pungent aroma of freshly cut grass, inducing an unrivaled euphoria!"

For Edith Pier of Middleton, a Wisconsin summer means the warm smell of sun-ripened berries.

"The berry fragrance evokes thoughts of fresh-baked pies oozing juice, and neat, shining jars of jelly standing in rows on the shelves of the fruit cellar, awaiting winter," she wrote. "The aroma of berries and dust, weeds and blossoms, grass and wild things mixes and swirls in the still air to create an intoxicating odor to be remembered as the smell of summer."

Some smells are a matter of opinion. David Mueller of Madison enjoys the smell of the summer algae and lake weed bloom on the Madison lakes. It takes him back to his childhood in the '50s, before the paper mills harmed fishing on the Lower Fox River.

But Tom and Sandy Dyer, Monona, list the Madison lakes in late August as one of their least favorite smells. They do love the scent of a freshly caught muskie, however, and inhale deeply to savor the spicy aroma of the Kabul restaurant on State Street.

Don't underestimate the power of smell to bring back the poignancy of a lost time.

A friend of mine died this past summer. A few months before her death, at her last birthday party, I had forgotten a sweater at her house. She washed it and sent it back, but I didn't put it on again until the weather turned cool in the fall.

And when I pulled it over my head, I smelled her scent and felt comforted. I know, logically, that I was mostly smelling her brand of laundry soap. But I still refused to wash that sweater. I wore it for months, with bread dough accumulating around the wrists and coffee stains tracking down the front, unwilling to give up that last, lingering trace of a friend.

LOOKING FOR HOPE IN THE MUD
Early Spring 1993

BLUE MOUNDS — Spring arrived here Sunday in the body of an early lamb that plopped onto the barnyard pavement around sunset.

Newborn lambs aren't the fluffy white charmers of the nursery rhymes. As he struggled to his feet, a thick rope of yellow mucus ran from his chin to the ground and his matted wool was stained saffron from the amniotic fluid.

Like the lamb, spring in the country is beautiful not for what it is, but for what it will become.

In the city, one warm day seems to send winter draining down the storm sewers. All that needs to be done, it seems, is to take the car to Octopus Car Wash and replace the skis with the bicycle.

In the country, the process is a lot longer and a lot muddier. People will tell you there is no spring in Wisconsin. There is, but it's mostly too ugly to photograph.

It started for us the day the road thawed beneath the last big snow and the snowplow truck got mired at the hideous bottom of the driveway, dumping a load of salt and inaugurating the mean season of intractable mud.

Our driveway has, for three weeks now, had the texture of French silk pudding — a quarter mile of vertical French silk pudding. Or perhaps, I thought one night, while slogging in from the road, it is more like one of those Blizzard shakes, the ones that have the crunched-up malted milk balls mixed in with the ice cream.

Or maybe I've got the food metaphors backward. The driveway did, after all, eat our 4-year-old. He went out to play wearing his knee-high purple boots and didn't come back. My husband heard a faint, "Daddy!Daddy!Daddy!" and found him sucked in up to the boot tops.

My own black rubber boots — caked with mud, manure and worse — have become an essential part of my look. I not only wear them while sloshing up to the car, I have to drive in them because the inside of my car has become as prehistoric looking as the outside.

Besides mud, rushing water is the second part of spring's eternal trinity. Rivlets join and fill the ravines with so much rushing water that a background roar fills the woods. We can be sanguine about the snow melt because we live on a ridge top and everything is racing away from us. But one of my valley friends reports seeing a giant, green, manure-scented foam mountain where the field runoff hits her stream.

All this moving water, it seems, inspired our well pump to do the same. One evening my phone rang at work, and the strangled voice of my usually mellow husband ordered me to, "COME HOME RIGHT NOW!"

When I got there he was kneeling next to the well shaft, baling water as fast as he could. The 10-foot shaft was full nearly up to the new wiring at the top. And inside the house, the baby was tearfully flinging herself against the window because she wanted to come outside to help.

Hours later, I waited fretfully to hear the verdict. My husband and a plumber friend had long since disappeared into the mostly dry well pit. Now it was midnight, and all I could see across the foggy yard was a shaft of light eerily projecting up into the gloom from the open hole. I crept across the dirty snow, fearful that they had been electrocuted or, worse, discovered a problem so expensive they couldn't bring themselves to tell me about it.

When I peered over the lip, I saw two men standing on bricks above the water. In the manner of men everywhere — men who signal their need to bond and talk by raising a car hood — they were staring down at the stubborn machine and talking animated boy talk.

"So, you brought a grinder."

"Yeah, they work great on nails."

"Yeah, I just got one too."

The next day, we slipped back another notch. The pump broke again, the truck threw a rod and my 4-year-old asked pensively, "Mommy, why does God make it snow when it's supposed to be spring? And what about tornadoes? And hurricanes?"

Then, suddenly, things got better. Our true friend came back and fixed the well for good, another friend lent us a truck and the sun finally came out.

Sunday morning, while we were doing yard work, a hoarse honking made us look up. A sandhill crane, the Korean symbol of luck, made three lazy circles above our house. And in a higher air above him, a pair of redtail hawks were joining and parting in a mating flight.

That night, the lamb was born at a friend's farm. An hour later I checked to make sure he wasn't the first of twins. He wasn't. And, thanks to a vigorous licking by his mother and his miraculous discovery of his own feet and his mother's teat, he was looking much better. Fluffy, even.

I could picture him weeks from now, frolicking with 500 of his about-to-be-born flock mates on the emerald fields of early May.

For, like brown mud and gray water, green hope itself is the third leaf of spring's trinity.

THE SWEET LIFE IN SUGAR CAMP
Spring 1994

MOVING CLOUD LAKE — Hot, smokey maple syrup sipped from a carved wooden ladle was for centuries the first food of the northern spring.

And even today, standing on the shore of a little northern lake that is still held captive by a dissolving crust of ice, it is easy to imagine the magic this warm, tawny nectar worked on bellies shrunken by the long winter.

Gathering at the sugar bush has always marked the end of winter and the infancy of a new Chippewa year.

Now, Chippewa people and visitors to this 17-acre lake on the Lac du Flambeau Indian Reservation will be able to participate in making maple syrup and sugar the traditional way.

The sugar camp of early spring is just one of the traditional seasonal camps Nick Hockings, a Lac du Flambeau cultural leader, and his wife, Charlotte, are building on the shores of this undeveloped lake.

The Hockings bought nearly all the land surrounding Moving Cloud Lake last year. Now they are beginning to build Wa-Swa-Goning, a village of seasonal camps that will show how the traditional Chippewa lived through the year. The sugaring camp will be followed by a spring spearing camp, summer camps that will have tribal members in native clothing demonstrating hide smoking, fish drying, weaving, wigwam making and dancing, and wild-rice drying.

The front part of the camp will be a place for visitors to walk through and take pictures of dances, native clothes, crafts, and the like.

Farther into the woods, people who would like to live for a while in the birch and cedar wigwams will populate what Nick Hockings described as "the spirit village." They will participate in the activities of a Woodland Indian camp of several centuries ago.

Hockings said he's had requests for such a place from tourist groups from as far away as Germany and Japan.

"They want a place where they can experience our culture," he said.

But Nick and Charlotte Hockings also see a need for their camp closer to home.

"Next year," Charlotte Hockings said, "we'll have it so the Ojibwa (Chippewa) children can come out to learn the culture. It's not enough to read about it in a book. They should experience what is a sugar camp."

Ironically, it was the heated controversy over one of these traditional food gathering activities — spearfishing — that helped reawaken an interest in traditional Ojibwa culture.

"When the culture was jeopardized, that's when things really got moving," said Nick Hockings, referring to a period in recent history that is now remembered as "the fish wars."

He said that treaty opponent Dean Crist "has no idea what he did for us."

This past week, the Hockings and some friends were running a small-scale version of the sugar camp. Charlotte and two women friends were hauling sap cans in from the woods while Nick was tending the blaze under the season's last kettle of syrup.

Next year, they hope people who want to learn the older ways of making maple syrup and sugar will visit Wa-Swa-Goning for a few days. There they will

GREETINGS FROM WISCONSIN

live in tents, chop wood for the fire, haul maple sap and learn to make the birch bark cones that are traditional for molding maple sugar.

"Everyone will leave with something," Nick Hockings said. "A couple jars of syrup, some sugar."

But more importantly, they'll leave with muscles stretched by sap hauling, hair scented by the fire, mouths that remember the sweet smokey flavor of maple water coffee.

They will leave having lived a ritual as old as spring itself.

MARTHA STEWART DOESN'T DO JELLO
Easter 1995

BLUE MOUNDS — With Easter fast approaching, I'd like to issue a little parent-to-parent advice about those Jell-O Dinosaur Easter Eggs. I modestly consider myself the Martha Stewart of Jell-O. But, perhaps I should back up a little.

There was a time when I would annoy my friends by making everything from scratch: I pressed homemade tortillas and rolled pasta, grew tomatoes, dried them and preserved them in olive oil. I still have the scald marks from the time I canned tomatoes while wearing a bikini top and splashed them into the boiling water while watching the 1980 Republican convention on TV. I realize now I was on my way to becoming the Martha of the lower middle class.

This, of course, was all B.C. (before children).

Those same friends now take snarky joy in going through my pantry and finding the Froot Loops, Little Debbies, and marshmallows that have replaced the semolina flour. These days, a balanced meal at my house is when we have fish sticks and macaroni and cheese (Kraft, of course; my children cry if I try to serve them the homemade kind) on the same plate.

So far, their diet seems to consist largely of food that doesn't look like food. My oldest is starting to eat the free-range organic chickens we raise ourselves, but he douses his chicken in ketchup, because he only became convinced it wasn't poisonous after eating McNuggets at McDonalds.

So, when my kids watch TV and demand candy in the shape of slime, scabs and snot, do I express my disgust? I do not. That last little bit of Martha-ness buried deep under years of Happy Meals raises its perky head and says, "We could make those ourselves!"

And we have. As native Iowans have always known, you can do amazing things with Jell-O.

So, when one of my friends spotted Jell-O Easter egg molds, she knew they had my name written all over them.

And, I must modestly say my first attempt at kaleidoscope eggs was a smashing success. When you add half the usual amount of water, Jell-O becomes sort of solid. And these eggs — layers of purple and red Jell-O, glistening and wiggling, with a toothy scab of undissolved powder marking the boundary between colors — were a raging success. The kids fought over the last one.

Then I spotted the recipe for dinosaur eggs. What a concept! Lime Jell-O made with half the water mixed with instant Jell-O pudding made with half the usual amount of milk to create an olive green base. Then you sprinkle it with cocoa to create mottling reminiscent of an 150-million-year-old egg. I knew they'd cause a riot among the 6-year-old oviraptors in the lunchroom.

And the first egg looked great. Unfortunately, I didn't heed the instructions warning to pour the stuff immediately. The pudding began bonding with the Jell-O and the whole thing congealed, making it glop around the opening to the egg mold rather than pouring through it. But, using Martha-like ingenuity and my vast array of kitchen paraphernalia, I decided to suck the stuff up in a turkey baster. But it jelled even harder and no amount of pumping on the rubber bulb would dislodge it.

So, using more ingenuity, I took the bulb off and tried blowing the stuff out, causing stress on several of my organ systems. About this time my husband wandered through the kitchen and he didn't even ask why I was red-faced and blowing olive-green slime out the end of a turkey baster. He just knows how creative I am!

Eventually, I conceded defeat. I'm sure even Martha herself has projects like this. I scooped the rest of the stuff into a ravioli mold (another relic of that bygone era) and tried to convince the kids that they were dinosaur bird eggs. They refused to touch them.

But studying excellent drab olive color created by mixing lime jello and vanilla pudding, I had the most marvelous brainstorm.

I could mix chocolate pudding with lime Jell-O and combine it with the olive green Jell-O/pudding. Then, using the same marbling techniques I once perfected on peach melba cheesecake, I could create — Yes! — camouflage Jell-O. It could be really big! And I'm going to try it as soon as I figure out how to clean the baster.

Moms don't know all the answers
Mother's Day 1993

BLUE MOUNDS — The chicks arrived last week and Lily was in 2-year-old's heaven.

"I hold them? I hug them?" she of the red curls asked, in her voice both husky and chirpy. Then she plopped in the hay in the middle of the fuzzy, chirping mass and considered.

"They miss their mamas?" she asked, frowning.

I sincerely doubt that these chicks have enough brain power in their fuzzy skulls to know their mamas, much less miss them. But I've been a mom for long enough to know the right answer.

"Yes," I said, nodding sadly, "they do miss their mamas." This set off another frenzy of hugging and petting so intense that the recipients may never make it to Sunday dinner size.

Of all the gifts my children have given me — I'm hoping today, Mother's Day, for crayon pictures, kisses and no fighting — their endless, sometimes hilarious, often unanswerable questions may be the most enduring. Travel, mind-altering substances, reading and religion are all touted for offering new perspectives on everyday reality. For my money, I'll take the questions of small children.

My children regularly demand that I seriously consider life from the perspective of newborn chicks, cartoon characters inside Nintendo games and God. Often in the same conversation.

The chief inquisitor is Ben, who is 5 and considerably less taken with the chicks than his innocent sister.

Ben has been around for a few seasons of chicks. He's seen them grow from fuzzy to motley to mean. He's traveled with his father to Grantland Packing before dawn on a cold November morning and watched intently as the lords of the barnyard were transformed into Thanksgiving dinner.

And, he has asked me this question: "Does God cry when chickens die?"

He also has returned home from a friend's farm with a bag of lambchops and excited stories about how he helped give bottles of goat milk to the orphan lambs. Later, as I cheerfully sawed and speared the tender little chops, he fixed me with a betrayed glare and asked, "Are those the lambs whose mommies forgot them?"

He, too, has stirred a piece of breast meat around and around in a puddle of ketchup and forlornly complained, "But the chickens were my friends."

In truth, the chickens were not his friends. He was afraid of them and thought they smelled bad. But his concern — his questioning of the essential meanness of life, the fact that we care for animals and then kill them and eat them — cannot be so easily dismissed.

Questions that are blown off with an "I don't know" keep coming back. And answers that imply that chicks and lambs don't have feelings teach the wrong lessons about life and our responsibilities to our animals.

I have found that answers with dinosaur metaphors ("We're the meat eaters, we eat the plant eaters") work, at least for now. But falling back on mainline science doesn't always cut it.

One night while reading stories in bed, Ben was so taken with an idea that he stood up straight on his pillow.

"Who," he demanded, "was the first mommy?"

I started to answer and he cut me off with an impatient wave, sure I hadn't grasped the full scope of what he was asking.

"No, when that mommy was a baby. If that baby didn't have a mommy, where did she come from?"

Well, I'm not always gracious about answering every last question. Sometimes I'm irritated at having to repeat myself, sometimes too cross about being late for school again to even listen. But I was ready for this one.

I used my college background in biology, my knowledge of his knowledge of dinosaurs and my background as a former science writer to paint a sweeping yet simple picture of evolution. I started with the little creatures that turned into fish that crawled out of the sea and ended with the monkeys that changed into cave people.

Ben listened intently and when I was through, I glanced at him with triumph, thrilled that at last I had satisfactorily answered one of his questions.

Ben looked at me and laughed.

"Mom," he said, between giggles, "do you really think we were monkeys? Monkeys have tails and live in trees."

Chastened, I trotted out the older story of Eve, Adam, God and the rib. He thought that sounded a lot more like it.

A few days later, Ben and his dad were driving somewhere in the pickup and Ben brought the subject up again.

"Dad, Mom thinks we were monkeys," he reported. "Monkeys have tails and brownish hair. Isn't that silly?"

Then Ben the inquisitor and Dad the agnostic shared a knowing, brotherly laugh about Mom and her silly answers.

GREETINGS FROM WISCONSIN

WHEN WE STOPPED HURTING LILY
Mother's Day 1995

BLUE MOUNDS — The day after Mother's Day will be the day we stop hurting Lily.

The circular saw in the orthopedist's office will cut open her casts for the last time. And what will emerge from those cocoons of fiberglass and gauze are the feet she'll have for the rest of her life.

These are not, you may have guessed, the feet that came with her when she was born.

In the hazy joy of her birth three years ago, I saw only her big blue eyes and the fact she was a girl. My husband, Matt, and our doctor noticed right away that something was wrong with her feet. They had the requisite five toes apiece, but they looked as if some clumsy tailor had taken a pair of regular feet and sewed them upside down and sideways. The sole was on top and they were pointing at each other.

Lily was born with club feet. This misshaping of the feet is one of the most common birth defects, occurring once in every thousand births. Its Latin name, Talipes equinusvarus, comes from the fact that ancients thought these children looked as if they walked on horse hooves. There are paintings inside Egyptian pyramids showing stylized ancient Egyptians walking on club feet.

I could go on.

As parents of children born with problems know well, you can acquire a ton of trivia while you're haunting those medical libraries. (This is a practice that I discourage, although I still have copies of medical articles on failed clubfeet surgeries in Russia.)

We started hurting Lily when she was 2 hours old. That's when Dr. John Whiffen came into our lives and started twisting those tiny feet into some semblance of normalcy. Meanwhile, Lily cried.

I don't want you to get the wrong impression about Dr. Whiffen. He has always been kind to Lily, her new, improved feet are his creations and we're very grateful to him.

It's just that we developed this strange relationship.

Once a week, for the first three months of her life, Lily and I would travel to the cast room of his office. There, I'd hold down my screaming baby and we, the doctor and I, would be nose-to-nose for a half an hour while he twisted and held those little feet in a new position while the plaster dried.

The first time I was so shaken by the experience that I nearly fainted.

I know all the reasons we did this: It's for her own good. She won't remember it. We're lucky she wasn't born with something worse. We're lucky we have insurance, good doctors and gentle nurses.

The logical side of my brain knows this. But there is a deeper, more primitive part of every mother's brain. And that part of my brain sends out a stronger, harder-to-ignore message: We're hurting my baby.

During those many drives home from the casting sessions, Lily slept from exhaustion and I puzzled out: Why? Why are we hurting her?

It wasn't so she could walk. A visit to Mexico or another less developed country will uncover lots of kids getting around on their club feet. Another doctor told us about treating a 21-year-old Salvadoran man who had become a baseball star even though he ran on the tops of his feet.

In my darker moments, I think that the real reason we have been hurting her is so she looks like everyone else. So that when she's older, and her peers have a more narrow view of what people are supposed to look like, she won't be so different. We're hurting her now to save her from a different kind of hurt later.

On better days, I know we're doing this because we want her to run and ski and ice skate and dance.

And so we sent a 4-month-old baby into surgery — an operation described to us as a "subcutaneous amputation." By cutting the ligaments and lengthening the tendons, the doctors were able to put the soles of her feet on the ground.

Those five hours were the longest of my and my husband's lives. But her second surgery, this spring, was much harder on her.

She had learned to walk in the interim and she thought her kidney-bean-shaped feet were just fine.

At age 3, she was smart enough to know what was going to happen when she went into the hospital. And she protested mightily.

Her tantrums — something she hadn't thrown much before or since — escalated into biting her own arms and throwing a final fit in which she attempted to strip in the hospital lobby. She was scared.

Following surgery, she sat up on the operating table and started grabbing at her feet and yelling. Back in the hospital room, her dad patiently explained that we had done this to her so she could run fast.

"But, Daddy," she said, angrily and correctly, "I could already run fast when I was a baby."

Now that the metal pins are out and the bones growing in their new places, she's feeling better about it all. In the here-and-now world of age 3, she can't remember not having casts. The long crawl across the yard to get to the sandbox has been replaced by an ungainly toddle on her walking casts. And she recently told me, "I think I better go to the hospital again."

When I asked why, she said, "I need some new presents."

So Monday she'll be going back for the last time. We've seen the new feet - all puckered with stitches and scars — and while they're not "normal," they'll do.

Later, we'll celebrate the end of this chapter in our family's life. Lily knows she can pick out any kind of shoes that she wants, and she's already given it serious consideration.

So if you see us in the shoe department Monday, we'll be the ones searching for the "Snow White shoes."

THE DROUGHT BABY
Spring 1988

BLUE MOUNDS —Bringing home a baby in the spring would be perfect, I thought.

Spring in Wisconsin is the lushest time, the babyhood of the year. In June, nature's equivalent of a baby's peachy cheek are its many shades of the color green: the vibrant blue-green of unfurling corn, the silvery-green of oats, the transparent green of new apples.

Except not this year.

This year the corn is brown, the oats gave up the ghost and the apples shriveled and fell of the trees.

This is the year that died in its infancy.

It doesn't even smell right. The air on a June night is usually heavy with the sweet fragrance of peonies and the winey perfume of the first hay fermenting in the silos. This year a scorched smell rises out of the fields. Light sprinkles this week only intensified the sour air.

I have a 10-week-old baby who's never heard rain banging against the windows.

Our alfalfa field is normally a sea of solid emerald, as anonymous as nature's Astroturf. But this year, the same way the skin of a dying patient shrinks to reveal the bones beneath, the alfalfa is showing the skeleton of the land. The plants are brown and dead where spines of rocky soil protrude down from the ridge, but still alive and green in the swales, where the heavier soil still holds some moisture.

There won't be any pumpkins for Benjamin's first Halloween. The patch that is normally a jungle of vines and yellow blooms is empty, except for the heartiest of weeds. My husband won't even go up to see what happened to his spring planting.

None of this would matter if only it would rain.

If only it would rain, we could salvage what's left of this season and start to look ahead, because as farmers, we known there's always next year. This blighted spring would fade, to be remembered in stories that begin, "Benjamin, the year you were born it was so dry that..."

But I'm scared about next year.

As I was driving home, burning gasoline, I heard a scientist on the radio saying that this is the beginning of the "greenhouse effect," a global warming brought on by years of burning fossil fuels. I've heard people talking about the hole in the ozone layer and wondering whether the destruction of tropical rain forests has somehow changed our weather.

Late on these freakish June nights, I listen to the baby coos coming from the small wooden crib and wonder if we've brought a child into a world where we've killed the springtime.

If only it would rain.

Haying season brings sacrifice on farm
June 1992

PARDEEVILLE — It's a rare June day in a Columbia County hayfield and all that is precious and deadly about growing up on a farm is here.

Nathan Bussian, 10, is piloting a Minneapolis-Moline M670 tractor around the field, its hayrake neatly fluffing the strips of alfalfa cut by his grandfather, Orlando Allen, who drives a second tractor hitched to a mower.

The conflict between the awful and the meaningful in this scene is stark: No occupation kills more children than farming, yet no other way of raising children is held in such high esteem, either by the dwindling number of families still farming or by the majority hungry for those elusive family values.

This conflict has left some farmers and safety advocates wondering if they speak the same language and searching for ways to prevent the tragedies that strike as predictably as haymaking follows planting.

Justin Isherwood, a Plover potato farmer who has written a novel about growing up on the family farm, was shaking his head as he left a recent conference on childhood farm accidents, held in April at the National Farm Medicine Center in Marshfield.

Isherwood said he was surprised at the safety experts who advocated laws that would ban children from farm machinery.

"Our value systems are different," Isherwood said. "There is a value system (on the farm) that isn't quite yuppie, that isn't up to speed with a lot of things."

Sister Miriam Brown, director of the ecumenical Churches' Center for Land

and People in Sinsinawa, said she also came away feeling she was hearing from two different worlds.

"They see it as the workplace," said Brown, a Sinsinawa Dominican. "Farmers don't think about it that way. It's the difference between an urban mind and an agricultural mind."

The agricultural mind, Brown said, "sees things as much more integrated, part of a whole, where everyone works together in the rhythm of the seasons."

Isherwood hated chores as a boy, but today sees the lessons he learned doing them as more important than what he learned in school. His children are 16 and 20 and they have also been doing chores since they were old enough to help.

"I farm with two brothers and all our kids work," he said. "We feel that's what makes our kids different, that's what gives us a special viewpoint on the world."

Thus, Isherwood and Brown would have seen the scene in the Columbia County hayfield differently than safety experts.

Farmers might first see the precious things, the pride on the face of grandfather Orlando Allen, who, having raised four girls, is clearly thrilled that one of "his boys" loves farming. And the joy on the face of the strawberry-blond Nathan Bussian, who has wanted to drive the tractor, said his mother, Laura, "since his feet could reach the pedals."

They would see the bond between generations, the performing of an annual ritual in a field where Orlando, 62, cut hay as a boy, near a wooded glade where the ashes of a beloved uncle rest.

As Nathan made his careful circles around the field that day, his brother, Mark, 12, laughed with their aunt, Barb Allen, who lives with her parents on the farm. Nearby, 4-year-old brother Andy, known to all as Pee-Wee, scouted the banks of Duck Creek for raccoon prints and scared up a newborn fawn.

But all that is deadly about farm life lurks close.

The Bussian boys, who also do chores on the hog and crop farm where they live near Columbus, are part of a profession that kills about 300 children a year and maims another 5,000.

Little ones, like Pee-Wee, are most likely to die falling off a tractor someone else is driving or getting run over in the farmyard. About four in every 100,000 farm children age 4 and younger die every year in one of these ways.

Older children, like Nathan and Mark, are most likely to die driving machinery designed for adults. And one study found that, in an average year, 16 Wisconsin children die in farm accidents. Fatal accidents peak in June and July, the haymaking months.

These aren't sterile statistics.

A few years ago, Nathan saved his grandfather, who had become entangled in the twisting grip of a power take-off shaft on a manure spreader being pulled by the same tractor Nathan is driving today. The power take-off is a rotating steel rod about the thickness of a broom handle that protrudes from the back of all tractors and converts the power of the engine to run machinery.

Laura Bussian said the boys' other grandfather lost two fingers untangling silage from a a machine on his farm near Columbus. And Nathan has already flipped the loader he was using to clean the stalls of the pigs he and Mark are raising to show at fairs this summer.

Laura Bussian is worried enough that she made the older two boys take a tractor safety class.

"Nathan is more cautious," she said, of the effects of the Dane County Extension class. "He's seen Grandpa go through the power take-off, so it's not like he doesn't know about the dangers."

But aware or not, Nathan is still a boy. His aunt Barb has "grounded" her nephew more than once for "hot-rodding" with the tractor. But she said her father always overrules her.

"He says that's how we grew up," she said.

The debate in the Bussian family reflects that national debate over farm safety.

The final recommendations of April's farm safety conference won't call for a ban on children in farming as European laws do, said Barbara Lee, assistant director of the farm medicine center. But they may call for parents to hire childcare while they work on the farm.

"One of the things we would like to encourage is that they think of themselves as being away at work," Lee said, adding that urban parents usually don't leave young children home to fend for themselves, while farm families often do.

Lee said her group wants to make risky farm behavior as socially unacceptable as smoking.

But others see the socially desirable aspects of farming as intertwined with the dangerous ones.

No other lifestyle, they say, gives children such a sense of being needed by those they love and such a chance to prove themselves.

Isherwood remembers clearly the year he was deemed old enough to cut hay himself. He was 8 years old.

"I still remember the feeling of superiority," Isherwood said, of steering the great machine through the alfalfa. "I felt like a Sioux kid who has gone on his first scalp raid. I felt superior to the others (the town kids). I was not their equal."

Things haven't changed much. A recent Successful Farming magazine survey found 65 percent of farm boys ages 10 to 12 were operating tractors themselves.

Others who grew up on farms don't think these are statistics that should make us proud. Lee Gross, a Dane County extension agent,, said that he, like Isherwood, was driving tractors by age 6 and haying alone by age 8 on his family's northeastern Iowa farm. He also remembers "doing a lot of crazy things" such as riding on tractor fenders and draw bars.

Gross taught tractor safety to the Bussian boys. But he also sees families who seem less concerned with their children's welfare.

"I've worked with families who were just overjoyed that little Junior is 10 and can finally drive the baler," Gross said. "God, it borders on child exploitation."

Some child development experts say no child younger than 13 has the cognitive abilities to make judgment calls while operating fast moving and powerful machinery.

Lee said that while some European countries have banned children from farm machinery, U.S. laws haven't changed since the 1930s.

Sister Brown believes that changing things other than laws would help. If farmers received better prices for their products, they could afford to hire adult help. And if they could reduce the "bigger is better" trend, farmers could use smaller and potentially safer equipment.

"It isn't all the farmers' fault," she said. "The fault lies in other trends the farmer doesn't have control over, trends this country needs to look at."

But until things change drastically, the terrible sacrifices of family farming will continue, a story as ancient as the seasonal rhythm of planting and harvesting.

This lesson, too, has been made manifest in this Columbia County hayfield.

Near the tidy red barn, just beyond where Nathan Bussian is raking hay, Orlando Allen can point to the spot where his own father buried the arm of a little boy many years ago. It happened in the 1920s, before Allen was born, but he and his daughters know the story like it happened yesterday.

The boy, 3 years old or so, was toddling along behind a hay mower when the horse team took a sudden turn and knocked him down. The blade sliced off the little boy's arm. Allen said his father, a neighbor to the boy's family, took the little arm up to the grassy area near the hay mow door.

"He put it in a fruit jar and buried it," Allen said, repeating the oft-told story. "It about broke his heart, the little hand and all."

Allen paused, then added that the tragedy did break the heart of the little boy's father, who had been driving the team of horses.

"He never forgave himself," Allen said, squinting past where his grandson is driving the tractor, his gaze drawn by a wooded rise above the hayfield. "He killed himself in those woods up there."

THE LOST ART OF LANGUISHING
Summer 1995

BLUE MOUNDS — Mononucleosis, like sex, is wasted on the young.

Ten days ago I learned that the reason I felt like weeping whenever a child or an editor asked for one more thing was that I was sick. I didn't hate my job or my kids or my husband. I was just really sick and I needed to go to bed.

So that's what I've been doing — languishing. Lying in bed in my 100-degree former attic bedroom, my spleen swollen to a Nerf-football size, a wet washcloth over my eyes, popsicles to ease my swollen neck, a little fan pushing humid air over my body.

It has been wonderful. Except for the phone calls. The ones from my girlfriends.

"You (name for a female dog), I wanna see that blood test," demanded one.

"It's not fair," wailed another, who is home with two preschoolers while her husband is off doing academic research for the summer. "I wanted mono."

Others have been calling to compare fatigue symptoms. They've had this long-running malaise, this feeling that they just can't keep up anymore. Could it be, they ask, mono?

It seems that the fondest wish of nearly every woman I know is to be ordered to go to bed and stay there.

It's just not as easy for modern women to get permission to languish. My historical novels are full of women who took to their beds for all kinds of reasons: nervous exhaustion, the vapors, vague and mysterious "women's problems." One of my mom's friends regularly used to have what she called "sinking spells," which required her to do just that.

Nowadays we have Prozac and ibuprofen and anti-stress vitamins and Tampax and all kinds of products that allow us to soldier on even when we feel rotten. And so we do.

I often feel like a human version of those broken-down jalopies that ferried the Okies to California in the 1930s. I've got a stove and a computer and frying pans tied on top and kids, family, editors, students and assorted others hanging off the sides. And even if I'm barely doing 30 miles per hour, my engine is close to overheating.

I'm not asking for sympathy, because nearly every woman I know is chugging down the road in exactly the same condition. (Men probably are, too, but they don't talk about this sort of thing.) The details of my friends' lives vary, but if they don't have kids, they seem to have twice as many job and volunteer responsibilities. And if they don't have jobs, they have more housework and kids signed up for everything from predawn hockey to midnight French lessons.

And this time of year in Wisconsin — when we cram all the swimming and vacationing and family reunions and sleepovers and gardening and projects into the three warm months — it all comes to a head.

What we all need is a nice, long nap.

I am still weak. And can't do much to solve these larger problems of our society. But as I lie here, the fan whirring and my kids dripping popsicles onto my inert body as they contentedly watch cartoons, I have figured out what I can do for my exhausted friends and countrywomen.

I've decided to sell my spit so others can languish, too.

WILD RICE HARVEST SIGNALS SUMMER'S END
Autumn 1994

MONICO — There is a certain delicacy to the annual harvest of wild rice.

Out on Spur Lake, a shallow pond in eastern Oneida County, the rice is so thick this year that the ricing canoes glide unseen through a watery thicket of tender green. The men poling the canoes are the only thing you can see from shore, moving like specters through the rice.

When they get closer you can hear the gentle clip-clip of the ricing paddles wielded by the person sitting near the front. The movement of the cedar paddles works like this: Bend the rice stems with the right paddle, sweep off the grains with the left, bend the stems with the left, sweep the grains with the right.

It's a mesmerizing motion, like watching a juggler or an orchestra conductor or a person skillfully eating with chopsticks. But instead of moving the rice from bowl to mouth, these sticks are knocking it into the canoe.

It's manonim time again in the North. Manomin (pronounced meh-NEW-min) is the Chippewa name for wild rice. Even its botanical name, Zinzania aquaticus, has a festive ring.

And manomin time is festive. The St. Croix branch of the Chippewa just had its three-day wild rice pow-wow last weekend. The Bad River band — which generally opens the ricing season because the rice ripens first on the sloughs where the Bad River flows into Chequamagon Bay — had its wild rice pow-wow in mid-August.

Traditionally, the ricing season marked the time when summer's bounty was collected to nourish people during the long winter ahead.

And in Wisconsin, ricing has evolved into an activity where law and tradition blend.

Although the activity is regulated like fishing and hunting, anyone in

Wisconsin can harvest wild rice. One boat on Spur Lake last week had Duane Poupart Sr., of Lac du Flambeau, in the stern and Tom Jordens of Minocqua in the front, working the rice paddles.

Like about 300 other Wisconsinites, Jordens buys a $6.50 wild rice license, which looks a lot like a fishing license, from the Department of Natural Resources. Poupart, a member of the Lac du Flambeau band of Chippewa Indians, is one of about 2,000 Wisconsin tribal members who gets a permit for off-reservation ricing from the Great Lake Indian Fish and Wildlife Commission, the Indian version of the DNR.

Last year, GLIFWC estimates that tribal people gathered 13,000 pounds from off-reservation lakes and non-tribal people gathered 24,000 pounds. The total tribal harvest probably exceeds the non-Indian harvest because such rich reservation rice beds such as Kaskogan and Mole Lake aren't included in the total.

Jonathan Gilbert, wildlife section leader for GLIFWC, said the agencies worked together to decide when the ricing season began and which lakes were ready to rice.

"Each tribe appoints a wild rice chief, someone in the community recognized as being knowledgeable about wild rice, who goes out over the course of the summer and checks on the lakes," Gilbert explained. "The rice ripens at different rates on different lakes, so you don't have a blanket opening day."

Generally, Gilbert said, river rice like that in the Lake Superior sloughs ripens first. Then the ripening tends to trend from lakes in the west to those in the east. This year the off-reservation season began Aug. 26 and will run to about mid-September. Gilbert said DNR wardens also assessed the rice lakes, but in most decisions "the state defers to the tribal rice chiefs."

Since the courts reaffirmed the Chippewas' right to gather, fish and hunt off reservation, other tribal customs are becoming part of the law.

"Tribes have had a custom of ricing for a day, then resting the lake for a few days to let more rice ripen," Gilbert said. "(Now) signs at the boat landings will say what days a lake is open or closed. It's really an interesting development that it's going from a cultural practice to a regulation."

Gilbert's agency has green rice buying stations set up at most reservations to buy wild rice for a re-seeding program.

Down at Mole Lake on Monday, warden John Mulroy had run out of money by mid-afternoon. He estimated that he bought close to a thousand pounds of rice that day at $1.40 a pound. The rice will be re-seeded this week, while it is still green and full of milk, into lakes such as Lac Vieux Desert that once had thriving rice beds.

About 40 or 50 prime wild rice lakes remain in Wisconsin, Gilbert said.

Others have been destroyed, he said, mostly by people hot for recreation.

As Gilbert explained, "Wild rice grows best in lakes that are 1 to 3 feet deep and have muddy bottoms. And people who live on lakes that are 1 to 3 feet deep with muddy bottoms hate them. You can't swim or fish in a lake like that. So people build dams to raise the lake level."

That kills the rice. Last year the agency replanted three tons of wild rice and is having some success. But, Gilbert said, "It takes time. You can't just throw out some rice and have a beautiful bed the next year."

Of course, not all the rice gathered is re-seeded.

Poupart and Jordens will take the 70 pounds they gathered on Spur Lake to a lean-to behind Poupart's home. There they will spread the grain on tarps to dry in the sun, then roast them in a spinning roaster to complete the hardening and drying process. Then they'll run the grains through a thresher. The rice loses about half its weight during this process.

But Poupart, a 34-year-old fishing guide who has been ricing since he was 10, said he has a list of people happy to pay $7 to $8 a pound for his rice.

Which brings us to another wild rice point. The cheaper wild rice you see in the grocery store is paddy-grown rice from (dare we say it?) Minnesota. Wild rice experts like Poupart and Gilbert say it has a flat, starchy taste when compared with the truly wild variety.

"People will see tribal people selling wild-gathered rice for $7 a pound and then they'll see the other stuff for $2.50 a pound and they'll say, 'Why should I pay $7?' " Gilbert said, adding that Wisconsin requires that paddy rice be labeled but other states don't. "Educated people should ask."

But, of course, traditional people believe the value of wild rice has little to do with price.

Francine Van Zile, who coordinates ricing for the Sokogan band of Chippewa in Mole Lake said the Chippewa valued wild rice because it was a nutritious food that saw her people through the winter. (One cup of raw wild rice has 120 grams of protein, almost no fat, and lots of potassium, phosphorus, calcium and vitamins.)

"Manomin is a gift from our creator, so it has a lot of healing power," she said.

Wild rice cured her bleeding ulcer, Van Zile said. She likes to take a half-cup of rice and soak it in water overnight until the kernels fluff up. Then she mixes in some milk and sugar and microwaves it and eats it for breakfast like oatmeal.

Van Zile recently made a gift of some Wisconsin wild rice to singer Bonnie Raitt. Raitt had a benefit concert in Chicago to help raise money for the Sokogan Chippewa's fight against a proposed copper mine near Mole Lake.

Raitt was thrilled with the rice, Van Zile said: "She said 'I'm going to take it home and cook it just the way I want it.' "That just cracked me up. You don't think of people like that eating your wild rice just the way they want it."

Turkeys the Size of Dobermans and Other Scary Thoughts.
Thanksgiving 1995

ARLINGTON — It would be tough to find a couple of better guys to talk turkey with than Mark Frank and Jim Mason.

The two tend UW-Madison's turkey flocks on the experimental farm near Arlington. And there's hardly a turkey question they can't answer. So to allow you to dazzle the relatives while grandma's carving the bird on Thanksgiving, we bring you the 1994 version of turkey trivia.

How big do they get, anyway?

It's a scary thought, but left to eat their way to maturity, the toms (those are the boys) of some breeds will grow to be 60 to 70 pounds. A DeForest guy who buys leftover poults (chicks) from the UW farm and raises them himself, Steve Trace, said that his birds get so big he's got to cut them in half to get them in the oven.

"They don't even fit on a Weber grill," he said.

Think about it: A bird the size of a Doberman motoring around under the control of a brain the size of an almond. Sounds like your basic talk radio host.

But before you start locking your doors, rest assured that commercial turkey growers never let their birds get that big. They concentrate on speed-feeding toms that will grow to be 30 pounds by the age of 20 weeks. Then the toms are slaughtered and made into turkey franks, turkey salami, turkey ham and all the other turkey products. Your Thanksgiving turkey is probably a smaller hen (that's a girl).

But should you hanker to see a turkey the size of Lassie, stop by the Arlington farm in March. That's the end of the breeding season, when the farm sells its breeding toms and when some of them top out somewhere around 60 pounds. Some people buy the big, old toms for meat, others buy them for pets.

"They let 'em strut around the barnyard, especially the bronze ones, because they look so pretty," Mason said. "We call 'em lawn ornaments."

And at least one regular customer gets his money back before the tom goes in the freezer.

Frank said the guy puts a big tom in the back of his pickup every year and then goes on a tour of the local taverns.

He'll tell the regulars that he's got a 50-pound turkey. And when they hoot and holler, he'll take $5 bets all around and lead the disbelieving drinkers out to the parking lot for proof.

"You think people would get smart," Frank said, "But they don't."

So how dumb are they (the turkeys)?

Pretty dumb. Maybe even dumber than the barflies.

So dumb, Frank says, that when they're young you have to cover up the wood shavings in their pens or they'll fill up on their bedding and not their food. So dumb that you have to corral the young ones under the warming light or they'll run off in a corner and freeze to death. So dumb that you can't play a radio near the poults.

Frank said he did that once and found fatal poult pileups in every pen. It seems that they would run to the sound of the music and pile up in the corner of the pen closest to the music, squishing the ones at the bottom.

Is it true that making (turkey) bacon is even beyond them?

Sadly, yes, although this is more a problem of anatomy than intelligence.

"You put a 40-pound tom and an 18-pound hen together and it just doesn't work," Frank said, "because the toms are just too big."

Those big breasts (his, not hers) get in the way and the tom tends to claw up the hen, leaving her vulnerable to pecking attacks from other turkeys who are excited by the sight of blood. (Again, we are reminded of talk radio hosts.) And anyway, artificial insemination is easier on the toms, too. Frank said the Arlington farm tried natural breeding but found it was too much work for the toms.

"That poor tom could only take on eight hens and he was just shot," Frank said.

So nearly all turkeys are produced by artificial insemination, but it's still an on-farm job, not the big business that cattle insemination has become. That's because turkey semen is only good for 24 hours.

You might want to share that with Grandma while she's making gravy.

What are those things on their heads, anyway?

The red, warty neck things are their wattles. That little black brush sticking out from their chests are their beards. And that long length of flesh that drapes over a Tom's beak and down his neck is called a snood.

Commercial growers cut them off, because when toms fight they pull each other's snoods. And, Mason and Frank said that you can tell the dominant male, because he's cocky enough to let his snood hang low. The other, more nervous males retract theirs into little snood knots on top their heads.

So, can you get attached to a turkey?

Well, Mason and Frank admit to being partial to the Small White, a breed of turkey that's all but extinct except for a small flock a professor keeps at the

Arlington farm. They're a chicken-sized turkey for a nuclear family: the hens top out at around 6 pounds, the toms at about 12 pounds. They're smarter and nicer than other turkeys, but most commercial growers aren't interested in them.

Beyond liking some turkeys better than others, Frank and Mason said they won't kill any of them. Thursday and today, dozens of the turkeys from Arlington are being sent to the UW-Madison campus, where students in the UW Poultry Club will slaughter them, clean them and sell them. Mason and Frank will help load them up, but that's it.

"We'll feed 'em and weigh 'em and care for 'em and love 'em," Mason said. "But we won't kill 'em."

But don't think you'll find these two eating Spam on Thanksgiving.

"I sit there at the table on Thanksgiving with a big smile on my face," Frank said. "That's when I get my revenge for all the nicks on my arms and legs."

ROMMEGROT MUST BE NORWEGIAN HEALTH FOOD
Christmas 1994

MOUNT HOREB — Representatives of the American Heart Association should not even watch Emma Lund make her famous rommegrot.

Plop, plop, plop, — in goes the butter, a pound of it in every batch. Whisk, whisk, whisk — in goes the steaming milk, full butterfat whole milk, of course.

And when the magic of Lund's whisking technique turns the mixture to pudding, it joins the earlier batches of rommegrot in the Nesco roaster, making a mountain of mousse as warm as a baby.

The rommegrot leaks golden rivers of butter that pool around the edges of the pan. And if that's not enough, well, there's a little pitcher with a heart on it that's full of drawn butter for saucing up the rommegrot.

No, not the meatballs in cream gravy, the lefse with butter, nor the krumkake, served at the Sons of Norway Christmas dinner would make it on a low-fat diet. But if it's so bad for you, how do you explain all the slim sons and daughters of Norway who are in their 70s and 80s, dancing around the Christmas tree like teen-agers?

Maybe it is the traditional decorations, the fresh greens of the pine forest trailing across tablecloths of snow white, lit by red candles stuck into birch logs. Maybe it is the chance to pray a Norwegian table prayer in Norwegian or to dance around the tree — little children in the center ring, older people around the outside.

Even the ornaments symbolize the homeland: Stars made from straw, tiny mittens knitted with even smaller snowflakes, rosemaled plates and little woven baskets, filled with candy and shaped like hearts.

Or maybe these hearts are helped by the sight of so many handsome women wearing bunads, the traditional embroidered wool dresses, each with a distinctive design of one of the valleys of Norway.

There is Marlynn Grinde in the black bunad of Valders, a valley that sent many immigrants to the Mount Horeb area. There is Olga Edseth in the elaborate embroidered bunad of East Telemark, Ann Nyhus in the blue bunad of Oppland, Marge Whitrock in the black jumper of Hallingdal, Myrtle Norland wearing the colors of Rogaland and several women wearing brocade vests that show they are daughters of Song.

While most of the celebrants are second and third generation Norwegian Americans, there are still some true Sons of Norway among them.

Thor Norland and Haakon Nelson, both 86, attended the same grade school in the Norwegian sardine fishing port of Stavanger. They separated in the fifth grade, when Norland's family moved to the country. When Norland was 16, he wrote to his sister in America and asked if she thought he would like the United States. In reply, she sent a one-way ticket.

In 1924, he moved to Madison and by 1932, he and his bride, Myrtle, a third-generation Norwegian American, welcomed their first child into the world.

Meanwhile, Nelson had also immigrated to Madison. He hadn't meant to stay, but some friends recruited him for an immigrant soccer team sponsored by Oscar Mayer. He played so well that his friends convinced him to stay.

Then one day, he read in the newspaper of the birth of a baby girl to a man named Thor Norland. He showed up to pay his respects.

We went to school together when we were boys, Nelson told Norland.

No we didn't, Norland responded, I didn't go to school in this country.

Well, I didn't either, Nelson said. Then, seeing that his old friend still didn't recognize him, Nelson went on to talk about their boyhood, about the time Norland was quarantined with diphtheria and Nelson climbed through the window to visit him.

Well, deadpanned Norland to his new, old friend, you haven't changed a bit.

And more than 60 years after their reunion, the two friends from Norway still laugh and laugh at the punchline, their eyes as bright as the silver buttons on their sweaters.

For all who make Christmas merry
Christmas 1992

MOUNT HOREB — "This kind of thing always makes me cry," said my friend Kate, who is generally not the weepy type.

We were standing in the doorway of the Mount Horeb Fire Station. In front of us, Santa was lighting the firehouse Christmas tree. Behind us, the Mount Horeb Community Band was playing "O Tannenbaum."

Inside the toasty firehouse, our 4-year-olds were playing tag through the lines of tables set up for the community potluck dinner and my baby had her candy cane sticky hands buried in a basket filled with warm Dalmatian puppies so young their eyes weren't open yet.

The Mount Horeb Christmas Firetruck Parade and Potluck is one of those idiosyncratic holiday traditions that make the holiday season special in this corner of the world.

Now in its third year, the silent parade consists of firetrucks from Mount Horeb and surrounding communities rolling through town at dusk, their lights flashing and their ladders festooned with Christmas lights. Santa follows in a bob-cat, its front end adorned with a swiveling deer head.

Some of this is sure to become part of our children's Christmas memories. When the kids get older, they may wonder what, exactly, firetrucks had to do with Christmas. (This is a union that makes perfect sense to the 4-year-old mind.) But I'm sure they won't forget.

My own Christmas memories revolve around midnight mass at St. Joseph's Catholic Church in Fort Atkinson. I don't remember many of the toys I got for Christmas over the years, but I can describe exactly the miraculous transformation the church underwent from somber Advent purple to Christmas green and gold.

Every town, it seems, has its people who help all of us keep Christmas in our hearts. They light the star on the bluff above Mazomanie, shoot off the December fireworks in Spring Green, hang the old-fashioned decorations in Boscobel's downtown and organize the carol singing in nearly every rural church.

And so to the firefighters and the wreath makers, the church decorators and the carolers, I propose a toast: Bless you one and all.